To RON,
God Bless

Rayfield Wright

#70
ROH '04
HOF '06

Wright Up Front

★

Wright Up Front

Dallas Cowboys Legend

Rayfield Wright

with
Jeannette DeVader

Editors
Frank Luksa
Dan Dunn

A Special Thanks to:

Bob Lilly for his candid photographs
www.BobLilly.com
and
Anne Kimbrough for her support.

★

For information address:
R. Wright Enterprises
P.O. Box 1865
Weatherford, TX 76086

Printed by RR Donnelley & Sons, Co.
Crawfordsville, Indiana

Library of Congress Cataloging-in-Publication Data.

ISBN: 0-9774401-0-9

Fourth Edition

Cover and book design by Jeannette DeVader.

Design consultation by Alan Glazener.

Dedicated to my Mother and Grandmother.

Mrs. Opel Wright and Mrs. Prentice Williams

You are the beacons of my soul that have guided me throughout my life. At an early age, you taught me the importance of respect and how to appreciate the victories and disappointments that I might face within life's challenges.

Abundant love, joy and peace surrounded your spirits and were generously shared. The experiences gained from your courageous lives were completely natural and born of God-given wisdom. Because you exemplified these principles on a daily basis, I realized their importance at a young age.

In the shadows of your light, I gallantly ventured through life with tact, perseverance, courage and integrity. Your love was expertly instilled; your teachings and ideals for living in this world have remained firmly by my side.

This book is a product of your souls. And with it, I express my deepest and lasting sense of love, admiration and esteemed gratitude.

With my love and God's blessings,
Larry Rayfield Wright

"In the beginning was the Word,
and the Word was with God,
and the Word was God.
He was with God in the beginning.
Through Him all things were made;
without Him nothing came into being.
In Him was Life—and that Life
was the light of all people."

John 1:14

CONTENTS

★

PREGAME

"Where's Rayfield?" I asked David Coffey, friend and retired CIA Trailblazer. "I'm looking forward to meeting him to discuss his book!" It was a hot Texas evening in August 2004. Tony Dry, a mutual friend from Abilene, was in town to make the introductions. I've known Tony and his wife, Janelle, for years because they make a very tasty salsa. Rayfield knows Tony because they are both faithful supporters of Disability Resources in Abilene, Texas.

"Rayfield won't be here this evening, Jeannette," Coffey hesitantly explained. "He's been involved in a very serious car accident. The paramedics are rushing him to the trauma unit at Harris Methodist Hospital in Fort Worth." Upon hearing the news, Tony immediately drove to the hospital to be by his side. I said a quick prayer in silence.

The accident occurred while Rayfield was traveling along a country road near Weatherford, Texas. At the trauma unit, he remained in critical condition for seven days with a severe concussion, several cracked ribs, a broken thumb (his first broken bone *ever*), a torn left shoulder and contusions to his chest, back and knees.

The wrath his body suffered that day was more damaging than playing against any of the great defensive ends during his career and more powerful than what the Doomsday Defense ever threw down on its opponents. By the grace of God, his recovery from the accident was successful and much quicker than what the doctors predicted.

★

Being a lifelong sports fan, my perceptions of professional athletes have probably been similar to those of the general public—gifted yet slightly overpaid, talented while remaining untouchable, proud and perhaps pretentious. However, after meeting and understanding the *real* Rayfield Wright, these unmerited perceptions left my mind faster than *Bullet Bob* Hayes once ran the 100-meters in the '64 Olympics.

At an early age, Rayfield developed personal skills through the Boy Scouts of America. Scoutmaster David Walker recalls him as being "one of the first scouts under my guidance to achieve 21 merit badges and receive the coveted Eagle Scout award." Mr. Walker admits that Rayfield was far from being a "hard-headed" young man. "He took an oath to be loyal, honest and obedient. He was a true survivor who has practiced these skills throughout his entire life."

Also through God's grace, Rayfield discovered a path that blessed him with an opportunity to attend Fort Valley State College, a small black school in Georgia. His college coach, Mr. L.J. "Stan" Lomax confirms that, "although Rayfield had an *intimidating and accepted meanness* on the playing field, he always carried himself in a dignified and stately manner off the field." Coach Lomax also declares, "Rayfield was an automatic leader who had the admiration of his teammates. Plus, he's never forgotten the folks who've helped him along the way."

★

There are more than 35,000 retired NFL football players in this country and Rayfield Wright is *one of only 13 players* in NFL history to have played in *five* Super Bowls. He was with the Cowboys when they won the title *twice*. (To date, the Cowboys have appeared in eight World Championship games.) After winning Super Bowl VI, it was Rayfield and his teammates who brought a rare, yet momentous smile to Coach Tom Landry's face as he was lifted off the ground in celebration.

Rayfield was under the direction of a stringent, military-driven coach whose *my-way-or-the-highway* approach to keeping the Cowboys' offensive line in order was not to be questioned. Coach Jim Myers recalls, "Rayfield's athleticism was a mystery to us. He came from a small school where he was phenomenal in track, basketball and football—a giant of a man both physically and morally." Being a coach who commanded superlative execution from his players, Coach Myers adds, "He was a coach's dream. Actually, Rayfield Wright *made a coach out of me*."

★

During his 13-year tenure as a Dallas Cowboy, and in spite of having four major operations, Rayfield was selected to appear in six consecutive Pro Bowl games, while earning All-Pro honors four times. In addition, his NFL colleagues and coaches elected him Offensive Lineman of the Year not just once…but twice. Only nine players in Cowboys' history played for America's Team longer than Rayfield Wright did.

Throughout his stellar career, Cowboys running backs cleared the 1,000-yard barrier five times. In 1972, behind the offensive line blocking, Calvin Hill became the first 1,000-yard rusher in the team's history when he ran for 1,036 yards. "Rayfield's career should serve as an inspiration to all athletes." Mr. Hill goes on to say, "In his first year as an offensive lineman, Rayfield took an ordinary position and made it high-profile by blocking against the notorious Deacon Jones, Carl Eller, Jack Youngblood, L.C. Greenwood, Claude Humphrey and countless others. The *Big Cat* could run, turn up, cut, block, catch... he was the best at his position."

Also behind the team's blocking, Hall of Fame legend Roger Staubach became the first quarterback in Cowboys history to throw for more than 3,000 yards in a single season. Mr. Staubach says, "Rayfield protected me in the same manner in which the Secret Service protects our nation's President... *with vigilance.*" It wasn't surprising to hear such a patriotic reference come from this Naval Academy standout. Mr. Staubach also acknowledges, "Rayfield was a self-sacrificing powerhouse both on and off the playing field. I am forever grateful for the immeasurable contributions he made not only to *my* game, but to the Dallas Cowboys." Both Roger and Rayfield retired from the team after the 1979 season.

★

Within a matter of weeks after his car accident, Rayfield Wright was inducted into the famed Ring of Honor at Texas Stadium. Rayfield, who entered the Ring along with former teammate and safety great Cliff Harris, was the first offensive lineman in franchise history to be so honored. (He insisted that the cast be removed from his thumb prior to the ceremony; his doctor reluctantly agreed and removed it.)

In February 2005, Rayfield was bestowed another honor when, along with Olympic great Mary Lou Retton, he was inducted into the Texas Sports Hall of Fame. In the audience that evening were former teammates Bob Lilly, Mel Renfro, Burton Lawless, Rodrigo Barnes and Robert Newhouse; and many family members and friends who looked on in glowing admiration.

★

In his personal life, Rayfield is a humble and gentle

giant—a person held in high esteem, positively regarded by his peers. Although mysterious and relatively intense at times, people should know this about Rayfield Wright: his family and his God are deeply cherished within his heart.

He has waited 25 years to tell this phenomenal story and some may wonder what qualified me to assist Rayfield in writing this book. Needless to say, I've asked myself that question many times. It has definitely been a tall order and one for which I'll be eternally thankful. All I can say is his decision in selecting me was typical Rayfield Wright. If he believes in something and prays about it, chances are he'll wrestle it across the finish line. It's true. My press credentials are not nearly as great as his faith in me. But in reality, which trait is truly most important in life?

If you're holding this book in your hands, Rayfield has tackled yet another great challenge. But I must caution the readers. The only white, powdery substance you will read about within these pages are the chalk lines on the playing field. Sex and scandal, bashing or bitterness won't be found here either. I'm not saying there has never been any craziness or controversy in his life. Exposing it to the public is simply not his style. What you will discover is an up front and candid story of tears and triumphs, fears and faith, and how *adversity and an innocent childhood prayer* provided his beat-the-odds inspiration.

This journey will take sports fans, Christians, coaches, promising athletes and anyone with a *desire to win* to the humble beginnings of his birth on the floor of his family home in small-town Georgia, through his valiant years at Fort Valley State College, to being drafted by and playing for America's Team—the Dallas Cowboys.

Nicknamed the "Big Cat," Rayfield's soul purrs like a gentle kitten while his faith, tenacity and valor are that of a hungry tiger.

Jeannette DeVader

5

The First Half

Growing Up The Wright Way

In the early 1900s, baseball was America's most talked about sport and was rapidly becoming the nation's favorite pastime. Football was being played at very few Ivy League schools. Sports enthusiasts in the upper class preferred expensive, flashy sports such as polo, golf, tennis and sailing. The game of basketball had yet to catch on.

During this time, Americans were facing a Depression and the World Wars were hovering on the horizon. The folks in small town Esma, Georgia, were working hard trying desperately to survive. Esma, located about 40 miles south of Atlanta, between Brooks and Griffin, basically had one thing going for it: the train depot. People who lived in the surrounding areas would come to Esma to catch the train to Atlanta and other places. The area was mostly desolate, open farmland and the houses were scattered miles apart. Very few families had cars, and those who did would simply, and graciously, offer rides to others. Needless to say, walking was the main method of transportation.

Families living in Esma had gardens where they grew vegetables, fruits and pecan trees. Almost every family had cows, pigs and chickens, so there wasn't much need to go to the store for groceries, except to buy flour and sugar. During harvest time, food was canned, preserved and stored for the next season. So food was not a big concern. There was always enough to go around, and

My great great grandfather.

those who didn't have enough found that others shared freely. Times were certainly different then.

Next door to Esma, in Orchard Hill, there was a Pastor named Judge Williams. He met and married a young lady named Prentice, daughter of Tom and Essie Matthews. This marriage blessed the couple with

My great great grandmother.

six children—Willie Floyd, Marvin (who didn't have a middle name), Rosa Lee, Myrtice Mae Francis, Opel Eleanor and John Henry. Three boys and three girls. Early on, tragedy struck their lives when Marvin died at 6 months of age. The cause of death was unknown.

Pastor Williams was a God-fearing man who had tremendous love for his family. The family understood that racism and cultural misunderstanding were certainly at its peak. However, under all the trials and tribulations during that era, they did the best they could in raising their family so their lessons would be passed from one generation to the next.

Living in Atlanta at the time was a man named Sam Wright. Sam was born in Cuba and worked as an auto mechanic. He was a tall man towering close to 7 feet. During his travels throughout Georgia, Sam met and later married Miss Opel Williams. He continued to work

10

as a mechanic and was later hired by the United States Air Force to work on planes. This new job took Sam and Opel to Washington, D.C. and then to New York City.

The couple soon welcomed their first born, a boy named Lamar Garfield Wright. Their second child was a girl named Earline Michelle.

When Miss Opel became pregnant with her third child, they moved back to Esma, where they lived with Miss Opel's parents. Sam Wright continued working as a mechanic and obtained another job driving an armored bank truck.

Shortly after this move, on August 23, 1945, World War II was ending and it was a hot summer's day in Georgia. The family was still living with her parents and "her time was near." The two men of the house were out working in the cotton fields, while the two women and two small children remained at home.

Severe labor pains struck Miss Opel that afternoon while she was hand-washing laundry in the back yard. Since the house had no phone, her mother ran more than a mile to the nearest house to use a telephone to call the doctor.

Luckily, her mother had asked Miss Pearl, a neighbor who lived a mile or so up the road, to stop by the house to check on her daughter. Now, back in the day, there were certain women called *midwives* who would come to the homes to take care of the sick and tend to women who were about to give birth. These midwives would comfort the patients and do whatever was necessary until the doctor arrived. They were important to the community, and certainly saved many lives. Miss Pearl was a midwife.

At around four o'clock, Miss Pearl approached the

house. Noticing Lamar and Earline playing alone in the front yard, she asked, "Where's your mother?" They replied, "In the house." Approaching the front door, Miss Pearl called out for Miss Opel. There was no answer. Upon entering the house, she discovered Miss Opel lying on the floor. Spreading a worn blanket across the wooden bedroom floor, Miss Pearl got Miss Opel somewhat comfortable just before she gave birth. With the baby still attached to the umbilical cord, Miss Pearl checked the vital signs of the child. Mother and child appeared to be in good condition. When the doctor arrived more than three hours later to administer to Miss Opel and her new baby boy, he found them both to be alive, in good health and, as he said, "with spirit."

★

That was my entrance into this world. Larry Rayfield Wright. Right there. On the hard, hot bedroom floor. The doctor didn't record my length at the time; however, I weighed in at 12½ pounds. I was blessed to be alive.

Now I don't know about you, but this had to be a very moving situation for anyone to encounter. But in 1945, coming into the world in this manner wasn't such an unusual circumstance because many people, especially blacks, were born in their homes instead of hospitals.

The reasons were plentiful: financial conditions, lack of transportation, the distance between homes and hospitals. I was lucky to have survived.

★

Earline acquired a life-threatening case of pneumonia when I was almost 2 years old. After this illness, she developed polio and was placed in

Earline in her braces. braces. Mother spent hours and days

12

traveling back and forth from Esma to Atlanta so Earline's polio could be treated. During those days, the spread of polio was rampant. Most kids grew out of it at an early age, just as Earline did. Luckily, she grew up to become a strong, healthy girl who remains without side effects.

Two years later and without incident, mother gave birth to her fourth child—another healthy boy named Phillip Perry Wright.

I experienced loss at a very early age. When I was 3, my father returned to New York City, leaving my mother alone to raise us. At the time, I didn't know that I would neither see nor speak to my father again until I was a junior in college.

But God and life prevailed. As time passed, and as I began to grow and develop, I would help my mother and grandparents plant and harvest crops in the fields. Whether it was working in the fields or chopping wood to heat the house and stove, I did anything around the house that needed to be done. I was a mere child and the work was *tough*, but that was all I ever knew.

For many people living in the South, hard work was an everyday chore. It had to be done. Of course, I went to school and attended church every Sunday and Wednesday night. That was a given. Most of my free time, however, was spent with my grandparents. They began teaching my brothers, sister and

Earline, Lamar and me. Our basic needs were quite simple.

me how to present ourselves, how to behave, obey and act around other people. Being a Pastor, my grandfather taught us from the Bible. We learned how blessed we were and how much God loved us. Not just black people—but *all of God's children.* We got to know Him, and put our trust in Him—in every way. My grandfather would say, "That through His son, Jesus Christ and the Holy Spirit, He will lead us, protect us and guide us through life if we simply have the faith to believe."

And I learned respect. Just as the word of God says in the book of Proverbs, "Parents should teach their children in the way they should go, so when they are older, they will not depart from those ways." This scripture is so true. I have seen many children and young adults refuse to honor their father and mother, and disrespect others. At an early age, I learned the importance of respect.

★

Mother and grandmother enjoyed their jobs.

One of the wealthiest families in Griffin at the time was the Cummings. They owned the land and house where my grandparents lived. One day they approached my grandmother to ask if she would be interested in becoming their cook and maid, and to assist in raising their four children. She agreed to this offer, and we all moved to one of the Cummings' houses, located at 833 E. Solomon St., in Griffin, Georgia. Our rent was $5 a week. The neighboring wood-framed houses were all very close together, and the community consisted of all blacks. Even though the house had to be heated with wood and coal, we thought it was a nice house. Some of the other homes in the community had gas and electricity. Ours didn't. But then again, we didn't know the difference.

My mother recalls a heart-racing event that happened to me as a toddler while living at that house. One morning I was playing in the yard with my brothers and sister when the neighbor across the street called mother over for a visit. Well, after a while, I decided to follow mother across the busy street. As I reached the middle of the road, I guess I just got tired and sat down. I didn't know much about crossing the street. I was just following my mother. All of the sudden a big truck came charging down the street toward me. The driver of the truck saw me and frantically began blowing his horn. As my mother told the story, neighbors began running to get me out of the way of the oncoming truck.

At the time we had a dog named Gal. A mixed breed of wolf and German Shepard, she was big and beautiful. Forever loyal, Gal was a great watchdog and always alerted the household whenever someone approached.

As I remained in the middle of the street, with the truck rapidly approaching, Gal leaped from the front porch and grabbed me by the seat of my pants. She pulled me to safety. I thank the Lord for that dog and her heroic actions that day. It saddened me when a man who thought she was a wolf shot her.

★

Our family spent many hours sitting on the front porch of this tiny house. Since we didn't have televisions, videos or Game boys, you would find our family spending quality time on the porch sharing laughter, love, fellowship and prayer.

It was on that porch I suffered yet another loss. One day, when I was 5, my grandfather and I were spending time together. As he got up from his chair, he immediately collapsed. He suffered a fatal stroke. That was such a sad day for me. Now with both my father and grandfather gone, my mother and grandmother were left to raise us.

My mother also began working for the Cummings family, cleaning, cooking and helping raise their children. It was a great arrangement. Grandmother worked for them in the mornings while mother oversaw the afternoon duties.

Even with the attitudes of racism running rampant in those days, the Cummings family displayed politeness and respect toward our family. As the Bible says, "We should do unto others as we would like for them to do unto us." No matter what the situation was, this was all I ever knew. This lesson certainly made a difference in my life and enhanced my relationships in the future.

The Cummings family opened our lives to many new experiences. With mother and grandmother working for them, they also provided small jobs for us children, such as cleaning their yard (it was a big yard with lots of trees) and arranging for us to deliver newspapers.

My oldest brother, Lamar, had another job after school and on Saturdays working for a man named J. T. Lawson. Mr. Lawson sold wood to families in the neighborhood. While in the fourth grade, I met Mr. Lawson and asked if he would also hire me. He looked at me and said, "Child, you are *too small* to do this job. You'd hurt yourself carrying these heavy tubs of wood." (I believe this was the first, last and only time in my life I was ever considered "too small" for a job.)

I was not about to give up. One day I noticed Mr. Lawson on the back of his truck filling up the #2 tubs with wood. (People would buy four #2 tubs of wood for $1. The boys would then carry the tubs to the houses.) I bravely approached his truck and asked, "Mr. Lawson, why don't you let me fill the tubs with wood while you sit in your truck and relax?" I guess he thought that was a great idea because he finally hired me. He paid me 25 cents a day after school and 50 cents on Saturdays. I was elated to have this job because I could now contribute to our family income. When I received my daily quarter, I would keep 10 cents and give mother 15 cents. On Saturdays, I kept 20 cents and gave mother 30 cents. I thought I had hit the jackpot! In those days, a penny would buy a kid a bunch of candy. One could even go to the movies for 10 cents!

★

Faith and Father Figures

With no man covering the house, grandmother felt it was her duty to take charge over the family. Standing 6 feet tall and known as "Big Mama," her words were simple yet firm and commanding of the respect all parents and grandparents deserve.

Big Mama was an early riser and, since I loved being around her, I would always begin my day with her. Our first chore was to start the fires in the fireplaces and stove to heat the house. Then we would get on bended knees and pray. She had an amazing relationship with the Lord, and constantly gave him thanks and praise. I always knelt down beside her as she prayed.

One day, at the age of 10, I knelt down beside the bed to pray our morning prayer. I quietly asked, "Big Mama, may I lead the prayer this morning?" She looked at me with a very powerful message in her eyes. (To this day, I have never forgotten that look.) She simply smiled and said, "Sure, son. Go right ahead and pray." Knowing how my mother and grandmother were struggling to meet the needs of our family, I simply asked God if He would, "Somehow give me the ability to help my mother and grandmother, to help my brothers and sister, and to help other people." When I finished this prayer, my grandmother asked me one simple question: "Son, do you believe in what you prayed?" I said, "Yes, Ma'am! I believe God will answer my prayer." She

then told me something that will echo in my mind and heart forever. "Keep this prayer in front of you, Son, and never let it go." That was her request.

My heart knew that God would hear my prayers simply because my grandmother constantly reminded us that "God hears our prayers and watches over us." And I did

Determined even at the age of 10. believe.

Almighty God has answered the prayer I recited that day. And it's still in front of me today. Praise God.

The material things in life were far from us but we had the most important possessions life had to offer: love, our faith and each other. Still without a car, my mother and grandmother walked to work every day. Regardless of the weather, we walked to school, to church, to town. It was the only life we knew, and it was good.

There was no question where our obligations were on Sunday mornings and Wednesday nights. We would be at Mount Zion Baptist Church. The Pastor, Rev. O. H. Stinson, was truly a man of God. My spirit moved each time I heard him speak. His heart and compassion reflected in his actions and in the words he spoke. He eventually became one of my father figures. Not one week went by that he didn't come by our house to pray for our family. His wife was also a very kind and caring soul. As the director of the youth and senior choirs, she came to understand and love our special family.

At the service each Sunday, I sat at the back of church with mother, who served as an usher. Grandmother was an Elder in the church and always sat toward the front in an area reserved for the Deaconesses. In the Baptist church, the male Elders (known as Deacons) sat on one side of the pulpit, while the females sat on the other side.

Mount Zion Baptist Church was built in 1927.

It was a natural experience for a young person to join the church through baptism and to accept Christ into their lives. Everyone in our family had joined the church, with one exception: Me. Family members and friends were curious as to why I, at age 12, hadn't taken that walk down the aisle to join the church and become a candidate for baptism. On several occasions, I heard my grandmother telling family members not to rush me.

When Rev. Stinson got to the point where he extended the opportunity for those wanting to be baptized to "Get up out of their seats and come forward," I always felt as though I was nailed to the bench. I couldn't move. It wasn't that I didn't want to join the church and be baptized. I did! My heart was so filled with joy and encouragement, yet, through my eyes, the aisle appeared to be so long and daunting.

★

Then one Sunday morning it happened. The doors to the church opened as Rev. Stinson prepared to close the service and something went over me and through me. I knew my mother thought I was just getting up to use the restroom, but I stood up, looked toward the front of the church, and focused in on my grandmother. My eyes remained locked on her eyes as I began to take what seemed like the longest walk of my life. I could feel the eyes of the entire congregation staring at me. I kept my eyes focused on my grandmother. Arriving at the pulpit, my face was covered with tears. My grandmother's eyes were also filled with tears of joy, and she had a big smile on her face. I will never forget that incredible moment. I can't tell you *why* I was crying; I just was.

When Rev. Stinson approached and laid his hands upon me, he asked questions about accepting Jesus Christ, the Son of the Living God, as my Lord and Savior. I cried even harder. When he turned me around to face

Big Mama on Easter Sunday, 1962.

the congregation, I noticed everyone in attendance seemed to have tears in their eyes. Sometime later I learned that their tears were expressions of love, joy and happiness for my family and me.

My grandmother's faith played a major part in my decision that Sunday morning. I was young—certainly not mature enough to fully understand the experience. I wanted to have the same close relationship with God that she had. She was a strong lady who had a calming peace about her that surpassed all understanding. Her love towered high above our personal needs and circumstances. Her faith provided strength and courage to endure. I wanted to experience the strength she had and I wanted to know what she knew. And I wanted it bad!

★

Two weeks later it was time for my baptism. Regardless of my fear of the unknown, I was looking forward to it. I watched those before me become baptized. It looked relatively simple. Hold your breath, get quickly immersed in the water, and come right back up.

When it was my time, Rev. Stinson told me to hold my breath for the immersion and he was going to bring me right back up. I was ready. At the time of my immersion, however, it felt as though I was held under the water *for a really long time*. It seemed like an eternity. That moment was long enough for me to have a vision. I saw a

Rev. O.H. Stinson

city—a city that appeared to have tall castles made of solid gold. Even the streets of this city were made of gold. There were no people in the city. It was empty. Never in my life had I seen anything like it. At first it appeared that my immersion was not as quick as everyone else's, but I'm sure it was. I didn't understand this vision, but it was real and extraordinary. Looking back on that special evening, it was unforgettable.

Weeks passed and the vision I experienced was weighing on my mind. My grandmother noticed something was bothering me and asked me what was wrong. My first question to her was, "How long did Rev. Stinson hold me under the water during my baptism?" She replied, "Not long. He brought you right back up." I then told her about the vision I experienced and asked her what it meant. She looked at me with her beautiful brown eyes, smiled, and said, "Praise the Lord!" She continued by saying, "Son, in time you *will* understand that vision. Ask God what it means."

Remember, this vision came to me at the age of 12 and it's still engraved in my mind to this day. Based on growth, prayer and maturity in understanding the word of God, I now realize what this vision meant. And I thank God for it. The image I saw was of the New Jerusalem—made clear in the Book of John and again in the Book of Revelations.

★

Christmas was a special time of year in which our family gathered, prayed and celebrated the birth of our Lord. It was a time of joy. Everyone would bring different kinds of food to our house, especially pies and cakes.

Earline, Phillip and me one Sunday morning.

(My mother's three-layer chocolate cake and lemon cake were, and still are, my favorites.)

One memory of Christmas was that, as kids, we each had our own chair. On Christmas mornings, we always found clothes and new shoes on our chairs. Toys were out of the question, but we didn't worry because we understood and accepted our financial situation. We were just thankful to get the new clothes.

Shortly after my baptism, one of the church deacons asked me if I wanted to deliver newspapers. I immediately agreed. Soon I had a paper route and was being paid. It was an all day job walking around the city of Griffin delivering papers. Walking those 10 miles didn't bother me because we needed the extra money.

At Christmas time this particular year, some of the kids on our block received new bicycles and wagons. It got me to thinking that if I had a bicycle I could deliver the papers faster and I still would have time at the end of the day to play ball. My brothers and I talked about building our own bike. We thought if we could find the right parts we could make our own bicycles, even wagons! The decision was made to start at a place not far from home called *the junkyard*. This was a place where people threw things away that were broken or discarded stuff they didn't want anymore.

At the junkyard, we searched here and there until we thought we had all the parts we needed to make a bicycle. Some parts were bent and old, but that didn't matter. We were able to straighten them out and replace some of the parts from one piece to fit into another. Eventually we had built our own bicycle. The interesting thing we discovered about building a bike was that if something were to happen to it, we could always rebuild it.

Most of the kids in the neighborhood had their own bikes and now we had ours. We were proud. And our bike was just as fast as the shiny new ones. Word soon traveled about our bike-building knowledge. So much so that whenever something happened to a friend's bike, they would always bring it to us to fix.

★

After finishing Grades 1-6 at Moore Elementary School, I transferred across town to Annie Shockley Middle School for my seventh grade year. It was twice as far to walk or ride the bike. Most of the transferred kids had to walk. There were buses, but we apparently didn't live far enough away to ride on them.

My eighth-grade education took place at Fairmont

High School. It was closer to home than Annie Shockley and, even though I still had to walk to school, I was now attending the same school as my brother and sister.

★

During this time, I was fortunate to join the Boy Scouts of America. What a great experience! I learned about serving the community and, through Boy Scouts, I was able to attend a two-week summer camp. Our Scoutmaster was David Walker, a great man who lived close to our house and loved working with kids. Just like Rev. Stinson, Mr. Walker became a father figure to me. Both gentlemen were instrumental in teaching me and

Boy Scouts taught me acceptance and respect.

leading me down the right path. I worked diligently during my time as a Boy Scout, and eventually earned the coveted title of an Eagle Scout.

As a boy, I never really thought much about my daddy being gone until one summer while attending camp. The camp was nearing the end and Mr. Walker had invited the scouts' fathers to camp that day. It was father-and-son time—a time to share the scouting experience with one another. On that particular day, after the fathers of all the kids had arrived, Mr. Walker told the scouts to "Go and grab your dad and show him your camp site!"

Suddenly, an awkward feeling came over me and I didn't know what to say or do. My dad wasn't there, and I was left standing completely alone. This was the first time I really missed my dad, or even *having* a dad. While deep in this thought, I felt a hand upon my shoulder. When I turned my head, I noticed Mr. Walker standing next to me. He smiled and said, "Larry, come with me to make sure that everyone gets to their proper camp site."

The feeling of missing my daddy kind of disappeared—even though I would sometimes wonder what my life would have been like had he stayed.

This was a turning point in my life where I began to grow up fast. I began to really *listen* to elders and mentors. I asked questions about everything. Through Scouts, I realized that the adult figures in my life were (and still are) very important. What they have to say is even more important. Their travels and life experiences certainly helped guide me throughout my life. Sadly, many adults leave their wisdom locked up behind closed doors. This knowledge is meant to be shared.

Sports Lessons Learned Early

Entering Fairmont High in 1958 was an exciting time for me, even though segregation remained a reality. Everything was separated. Whites had their schools; blacks had theirs. There were white restrooms and black restrooms. There were water fountains for whites and there were water fountains for blacks. In riding any form of transportation, blacks still had to sit in the back. There was never a time when blacks and whites would get together to play sports or anything else. That was the way of life in this country, especially in the South. I never really understood this environment because I always believed that we were all children of God.

Around this time, I became very interested in sports, especially basketball. We made a basketball goal (with stuff from the junkyard) in our back yard, which became the after-school hangout for the neighborhood kids. The younger kids played only if there weren't enough big guys to complete a team.

Initially I enjoyed sitting on the ground watching the big guys play. They were awesome. After weeks and months of studying the big guy's moves, I thought

I was ready to play. When given the chance to play and shoot the basketball, I tried to emulate the bigger kids. Sometimes it worked, but most of the time my shots were denied. Nicknamed "Silver," my oldest brother, Lamar, was a great player. He saw my interest in the game and began teaching me more about it. He kept saying, "You have to develop your own style, Larry." Later in my life, this fundamental lesson became incredibly useful to me.

Most kids living in Griffin played sports and the big guys always taught the younger kids how to play. All the major sports—basketball, football, baseball, volleyball and even track—were learned, practiced and played. (Golf had yet to catch on in Griffin.) As the seasons changed, we played that sport. My biggest challenge in sports was my height, and the fact that I was such a skinny kid. The bigger kids, especially Silver, didn't want me to get hurt. He was always protecting me.

At Fairmont, I tried out for the football team and, incredibly, Coach Hiram Whitaker didn't let me play. *I didn't make my high school football team!* It's not that I couldn't play the game. It was because I was such a tall and skinny

Coach Hiram Whitaker kid. There were some big, physical players on that team and, even though I played in the neighborhood with most of these guys, Coach Whitaker thought I might get hurt. So I became one of the ball boys—which was great! It kept me near the action.

As it remains in the South today, players and fans took the game of football seriously. We had several rivals in nearby cities, as most teams often do. There are certain opponents in each sport that you have a strong desire to defeat. Our greatest rival was from the town

of McDonald. Mother's oldest sister, Myrtice, lived in a smaller city named Locust Grove, and all the kids from Locust Grove went to McDonald. Aunt Myrtice had eight children. One of her sons, my cousin "Bubba," was captain of the McDonald football team.

One particular game between Fairmont and McDonald was for the championship. Both teams were playing great until the unexpected happened. Fans from McDonald High began getting rowdy and violent. The next thing I knew, there was a fight on the field between two players. Fans poured from the stands onto the field, causing a horrifying scene. We had a great running back named J.B. Murphy, who was a senior and had his sights set on playing college ball. When the fight was over, J.B. had been stabbed with a knife by one of the fans. He ended up losing a kidney and never played another game of football.

I know how intense one can get as a player and as a fan. However, fans should never come onto the playing field to confront a player. And players should settle their differences with other players while on the playing field.

Lamar in 1962.

★

After football season ended it was on to basketball. I tried out for the team and made it! It was thrilling, and I was now a high school athlete. Our team consisted of several of my cousins and my brother, Lamar. At 6-9, he was our tallest player. I was only 6-foot at the time, but we had one great year of playing the sport together.

The next year, Lamar got into trouble at school and was suspended. He went to live with Aunt Myrtice, which meant he had to attend McDonald High, our greatest rival. He joined their basketball team, so we found ourselves competing against one another. I thought I knew what rivalry and competition were, but playing against my brother created fierce competition. Each time we played, fans from both cities came out to see the match-up between the Wright brothers. It was heated competition. Brother against brother.

Left to Right: *Willie Simmons, James Walker, Leroy Blanton, Larry Wright, Damon Coggins and Charles Daniels were seniors on the 1962 Fairmont High School basketball team.*

I worked especially hard developing my skills in basketball. During my junior year in high school, I was voted to the All-Star team. My senior year was just as exciting. Sports became such a passion for me that I went out for football again and finally made the team as a tight end. Football was great, but basketball was my chosen sport.

Honestly, I didn't play much football in high school until my senior year, but I gave the game all I had. My focus remained on basketball. My athletic abilities began to draw attention from some big colleges that had excellent basketball programs. I remember traveling to Atlanta to play in the High School All-Star Game, which included players from throughout the state of Georgia.

One of the All-Star players in Atlanta that night was Walt Frazier. We were on opposite teams. He played an outstanding game and so did I. He was a guard and I was playing forward. Walt finished the game with more than 30 points and took home the Most Valuable Player award. I came in second with more than 20 points and several rebounds. Walt's performance in that game captured my attention. He had perfected a one-hand set shot that he could hit from the half-court line. Even though I had a good jump shot, most of my points were scored around the basket.

Basketball was my goal.

Walt was one of the best guards I had ever seen. He later joined the New York Knicks of the National Basketball Association. He was nicknamed "Clyde" after the famed folk-hero robber Clyde Barrow from the film *Bonnie & Clyde*. His success as a professional basketball player continued for many years thereafter.

I received several basketball scholarship offers, with the most exciting one coming from Loyola University in Chicago, which was developing a high-profile basketball program. Several NBA players have attended Loyola— even before my time. Unfortunately, these weren't full scholarships, and my family didn't have the financial resources for me to go to college.

My senior year was ending and, since Lamar was suspended and Earline missed some grades because of her polio, I was going to be the first one in our immediate family to graduate from high school. Although my dream was to attend college and play basketball, I remained uncertain about my future. With the financial challenges we faced, I couldn't see where additional funds would come from to make this dream a reality. All I could do was to say my daily prayer to God.

★

Recruited

Among the events at Fairmont High was an annual Career Day for seniors. Leaders from different businesses and industries would come to the school and present career opportunities to the senior students.

I joined my classmates in the auditorium for Career Day and sat there getting very confused. There were several things running through my mind and I couldn't decide what I wanted to do. Understanding the trials my family was suffering, I wanted to do something to help them. My brothers and sister were trying to graduate from high school and they needed some support. Although I wanted to continue my education and play basketball, I didn't have the necessary funds to do so. Clothes were also a problem. When I graduated from high school that year, I borrowed a black suit from Morris Stroud, my cousin, who stood more than 3 inches taller than me. Can you imagine the fit? Anyway, Morris was a great athlete who went on to play tight end for the Kansas City Chiefs.

I never mentioned my concerns to anyone—only in my private prayers to God. The prayer I prayed with my grandmother at the age of 10, where I had asked

God to "bless me with the ability to help my mother and grandmother, my brothers, sister and others," was still in front of me.

Career day was almost over and I was unimpressed with the business opportunities presented to me. As the next speaker began his approach to the podium, my eyes remained focused on him. There was something *dynamic* about the way this man carried himself. When he began to speak, I immediately realized that this was the type of man I wanted to become. In my mind, everything about him was perfect—the way he walked, talked and dressed. He was a Captain in the Air Force. I would soon discover my new career. Or would I?

The Captain was there to recruit students to join the service. After the program, students gathered around the speakers of their choice to ask questions. Approaching the Captain, I said, "Sir, my name's Larry Wright. I'm interested in joining the service and furthering my education. I'm also a basketball player." I was curious to see if he had a program that would satisfy my interests.

He replied, "Well, you certainly look like you play sports! And there is a program in special services where you can continue your education and participate in sports." As he talked about the program, I became extremely interested. I told him that I might have some other friends that might be interested in this opportunity.

This happened in 1963, when the world was at peace. It had never occurred to me to join the service, but I learned about the Buddy–Buddy program where several individuals could sign up and go through basic training camp together. After basic training, one could decide what part of the service they would like to pursue. I already knew what my interests were—education and the opportunity to play basketball.

Like me, several of my friends didn't know where they were going after graduation. I told them about my conversation with the Captain, and that it would be a great opportunity to further our education—and perhaps even to play sports. They thought this was a great idea, so we all signed up to join the military. My mother and grandmother weren't too happy about hearing this news but, since there wasn't a war taking place at the time, they agreed with my decision.

After graduating that June, my friends and I traveled to Atlanta to take the physical examination. It was *particularly thorough*, but we all passed. Our next steps were to be sworn in and prepare for basic training. Training was to begin five months later, after Thanksgiving.

The townspeople of Griffin knew of our plans to join the service. In those days, good job opportunities were difficult to come by—especially

Searching for stability at 17 years old.

for blacks living in a small community. Most graduates before me attended college, joined the service or moved to a larger city to get a good job. If one graduated from high school and had the opportunity to go to college, he or she most likely became a teacher in Griffin or the surrounding area. Achieving this was considered a success.

In life, based on our experiences and willingness to share with others, we all are teachers. I would have been satisfied becoming a teacher, but I *desired* to be a professional basketball player.

John Willis, my cousin, went on to coach high school football.
His insight jump-started my football career. Thank you, Bubba!

★

A few months before basic training, as I approached my 18th birthday, I received a telephone call from my cousin Bubba. He was in his second year at Fort Valley State College, located about 60 miles from Griffin. Bubba was such a great football player at McDonald High School that he received a scholarship from Fort Valley, along with a government grant to pay the difference in tuition fees.

Bubba was a captain on the football team. He felt he could talk to his coach about my athletic ability and maybe the coach would offer me the same kind of scholarship and grant. I said, "Bubba, you know that I've volunteered for the Air Force. I'm leaving for basic training in three months!"

As you can imagine, nothing much stopped Bubba's spirit. Not even my words. Regardless of what I said, Bubba was determined to talk to his coach—a man by the name of L.J. "Stan" Lomax—on my behalf.

Coach Lomax was the new football and basketball coach who was hired to help build the athletic program. True to his word, Bubba spoke with Coach Lomax about my athletic abilities, telling the coach that I was able to play both football and basketball, and that he should give me a call.

After talking briefly with Coach Lomax on the telephone, I was invited to Fort Valley for a visit. Having never been on a college campus before, I thought this would be a great opportunity. At the same time, I could also visit with Bubba. I arranged for a bus ticket on Greyhound from Griffin to Macon—about 15 miles from the city of Fort Valley. Bubba arranged for me to be picked up and brought to the campus.

★

I didn't know what to expect upon my arrival in Fort Valley. It was just as small as Griffin was, maybe even smaller. We went straight to the college. At the entrance of the college, there was this huge arch across the entrance that read "Welcome to Fort Valley State College." Incredibly enough, it felt as though this arch reached out, extended around my soul and embraced me. I felt completely welcome and at peace. We drove to the gym where the coaches had their offices. Riding through the campus and seeing the students and all the buildings made me feel special. It was such a beautiful campus. I couldn't believe what I was seeing.

Waiting in the gym with Bubba were some coaches. After our brief greetings and introductions, we went to the athletic department to meet Coach Lomax. As we passed the basketball court, I had to stop to look inside. It was big! There were some college players on the court shooting the ball around. Man! I desperately wanted to put on my tennis shoes and play with them.

When we reached the athletic department, Bubba introduced me to other coaches and the athletic director. After the introduction to Coach Lomax, we sat together talking about my family, athletic ability, grades and my goals in life. I expressed to him that I would love to attend Fort Valley, but I had a "little situation." When he inquired about this, I told him that I had, along with several of

Mrs. Frambo loved 'her' athletes.

my friends, volunteered for the Air Force. I further explained that given our financial conditions, I thought this would be the best thing for me and that it was a commitment I had made. To be honest, I didn't have any other career choices. For some reason he appeared unconcerned about my "situation."

After we talked for a while, he took me on a tour of the campus and introduced me to several students and instructors. One of the buildings we went to was the cafeteria. It was close to lunchtime, so we ate. I was introduced to a lady named Mrs. Frambo, the head of the cafeteria, who undoubtedly took great care of 'her' athletes.

Coach Lomax continued asking about my education and whether or not I liked Fort Valley. What else could I say except that "it was great! I would love to attend this school, but there is this situation that I have." He still didn't seem worried by my situation.

At the end of the day, Coach Lomax offered me a scholarship and a grant to help pay the rest of my tuition. He also told me that I would have a job on campus.

This happened on a Friday and many students headed home for the weekend. Bubba was going to Atlanta and had to drive through Griffin to get there. Instead of riding the bus to Griffin, I caught a ride with him and his friend. We talked the entire way about my possibilities of attending Fort Valley.

When I arrived home, I told my mother and grandmother about the entire visit, yet I was burdened about the decisions in front of me. As usual, my grandmother told me to pray about it. We all prayed that night. They were as excited as I was, but I didn't know how things could (or would) work out.

When Coach Lomax continued to call about attending Fort Valley, I finally told him, "Mr. Lomax, you need to understand my situation. If I were to attend college, you will have to come to Griffin and talk to a few people about it." When he asked "whom," I told him "my mother and grandmother, my minister, my scoutmaster and the recruiting officer from the Air Force." He said he would be happy to come and speak with them and to let him know the time and place. He would be there. I went to work arranging everyone's schedule for Coach Lomax's visit to Griffin. He showed up just as he said he would.

In those days, when adults would get together to talk, for whatever reason, the children were sent outside until the adults were finished. Out of constant respect for my elders, and even though they were talking about *my* life and future, I went outside and waited on the front porch. By this time, that rickety old porch was a stage where many of my life-altering changes had debuted. Little did I know that it would be the setting for many more to come.

Several hours passed while I remained on the porch uncertain of what was taking place inside. The front door finally opened and my mother and grandmother appeared. They were both crying. At first, I didn't know whether to cry along with them or become upset. Then the recruiting officer came out and approached me. He told me that I could go to college. I then began to cry.

Before leaving that night, the recruiting officer made one important point very clear to me. He sternly told me that "if, for whatever reason, you drop out of school or flunk out, you will *immediately* be drafted into the United States Army." I made a firm commitment to everyone that, if given this incredible opportunity, I would stay in school until I received my college degree.

Coach Lomax explained the scholarship and grant programs, and said he would help me with additional financial assistance. He made three commitments: First, the scholarship would be for four years; second, both a student educational assistance program and government grant would be available (I would have to pay this money back after graduation.); and third, he would help me get a student job on campus so I would have some financial help. Interestingly enough, the campus job turned out to be in the school cafeteria serving students and cleaning up. (I thought that was cool. I didn't have to worry about how I was going to eat.)

During this time, my other situation was weighing heavily on my mind, and not just because of my commitment to the Air Force. I was deeply concerned about my friends that I had persuaded to join with me. That was a tough one. In the end, they wished me all the best as they entered the service without me. Today, whenever I travel home, they remind me of the situation and we joke about it.

Now keep in mind that joining the service is a great opportunity for those who are unable to continue their education by going to college. Facing my choices at the time, and given all of my circumstances, I chose the path I thought was best for my family and me.

Fort Valley was one of three predominately black Georgia colleges, along with Savannah State and Albany State. These colleges were on quarter systems rather than semesters.

By the time things worked out for me to begin college, in September 1963, it was too late to join for that quarter, so I had to wait until the second quarter began. So for a few months I worked in Griffin at one of the textile mills. My first college quarter began in January 1964. I couldn't wait! Basketball season had already started when I joined the team. I didn't know how the team would respond to me or how I would be treated. Luckily, Coach Lomax told the players that I would be joining them after Christmas. When I arrived, they welcomed me as though I had been with them since the beginning of the season. I was eager to compete at the college level. After a few weeks, I became a starter at the forward position. Finishing the season as a starter, I was on top of the world.

College teammates (l-r) Bill Ingersoll, Edward Robinson, Leonard Laster,Ed Carter and me.

When the season ended, I began to focus on my grades. Being a quarter behind, I overloaded my class schedule with 18 to 20 hours instead of taking the average 12 hours. Doing so didn't leave me much time to play around. I was always studying, even during most weekends. The perception of athletes always partying didn't apply to me. I was focused on school and sports.

"Where are you, Larry?"

After school was out that June, I headed home to Griffin to begin my summer job. I desperately needed to make some extra money to buy clothes and help my family as much as I could. I was blessed to get my job back at the textile mill, and I was prepared to make some pretty good money.

Within the first week of my return, and after the long walk home from the mill, mother met me on the porch. She said, "Coach Lomax called and wants you to call him." She didn't tell me what the call was about but she said that he "sounded rather upset." I didn't know what was going on, so before supper that evening I placed a call to him.

When he answered, I could sense his frustration. He asked, "Why aren't you at spring football practice, Larry?" I was shocked! I replied, "Coach, I didn't know that I was supposed to be at spring football practice." (After all, I had a basketball scholarship!) He then said something that shocked me even more. He said, "Son, you have an *athletic* scholarship, which requires you to play two sports! You need to be here for football training!"

I quit my job at the mill and went back to Fort Valley to begin football practice. I didn't know what position he wanted me to play. And it really didn't bother me to play football even though it wasn't my first choice. I was a good athlete who could play almost any position on the team. That's what I did in my childhood. When it was football season, sometimes I was the quarterback, receiver, kicker and pass rusher—almost every position on the team.

★

At Fort Valley, the first position I played was free safety. Then I became a punter, a defensive end and finally

a tight end. I performed well at all positions and enjoyed playing football and helping the team. Still, most of my enjoyment came from playing basketball.

During this particular training camp, I was punting the ball, making tackles and intercepting

I did anything I could to help the team.

passes as a free safety, sacking quarterbacks as a defensive end and scoring touchdowns as a tight end. In basketball, I was scoring points and getting rebounds. I began making a name at Fort Valley and was quickly becoming recognized as one of the top athletes in the Southern Intercollegiate Athletic Conference (SIAC).

I didn't know where my abilities were going to take me, but I began to seriously concentrate on becoming a great player in both sports. I was hoping to develop my talents to excel enough to reach the professional ranks. Maybe then I would have an opportunity to try out on that level.

★

In the meantime, my brother Lamar had gotten himself together and was graduating from McDonald High School. I went to Coach Lomax and told him about my brother and his basketball talents. I asked Coach if he would consider bringing Lamar to the Fort Valley basketball team. Lamar was much taller than me and he could really play the game. I knew that, if given the chance, he could help the basketball program.

My brother, Lamar (r), taught me the importance of heathly competition.

Eventually, Lamar came to Fort Valley and made the basketball team. Being our tallest player, with Lamar it was said that Fort Valley had its own Wilt Chamberlain. Wilt was a 7-1 NBA all star, drafted in 1959 from Kansas University by the Philadelphia Warriors. I knew that if Lamar stayed with the program he might get an opportunity to follow in Wilt's size 14 shoes.

★

I always wondered why Lamar was dismissed from high school but the subject was never discussed. Knowing

Mr. Daniels, the principal, he must have had a good reason for what he did. When the incident happened, I was very concerned about it and angry with Mr. Daniels. On the other hand, I knew Mr. Daniels must have had justification behind his decision.

Shortly after Lamar came to Fort Valley, at the beginning of my sophomore year, my mother received

a call from Mr. Daniels. He had spoken to a gentleman who said he wanted to "help a certain college student who needed some financial aid." Mr. Daniels recommended me for the assistance. One can imagine the shock my mother felt!

Mr. Daniels was a fair man who could keep a secret.

"Why did you recommend Larry?" she asked.

"Larry was a great student and I can see that he is determined to do something important with his life," he said. "I know Larry needs a little financial help. And this gentleman received help when he was trying to finish school. He now wants to pass that assistance on to someone else."

What a blessing from God! During my entire college career, on the first of every month, I received a $50 bill in the mail. It arrived in an envelope postmarked from Griffin but never carried a return address. Even though we tried to find out the identity of this anonymous gentleman, Mr. Daniels would never reveal his name. All we learned was that he was a white man from Griffin with a military background. My mind and heart always took me back to the one person who may have done this —the recruiting officer from the Air Force. I never knew for certain, but I desperately wanted to discover who was being so generous to me. His identity still remains a mystery.

Mr. Daniels told me that the only request this gentleman made was that "if someday, Larry ever finds himself in a financial position to help another student get through college, that he seek them out and return the blessing." I promised Mr. Daniels that "I would most certainly honor this gentlemen's request and perform this kind and generous action!" To this day, I have kept my commitment to assist select college students in their educations, and will continue to do so.

★

During the next two quarters, I was studying hard, passing my classes, working on campus and improving my football and basketball techniques. This devotion got me selected to the All-SIAC Team in both sports.

That summer I attended summer school to make up the classes I missed my first quarter. This also gave me the opportunity to practice and involve myself in a weight-training program designed by Coach Lomax. I always enjoyed working out and lifting weights to strengthen my body, but I had never tried to "max out" through weight lifting. During these workouts I noticed that lifting weights was great but, if you over-lifted, you built muscle while reducing your speed and quickness. I wanted to be strong but, since basketball requires quickness, I wanted to find a balance between strength and speed. I discussed these concerns with Coach Lomax, and he agreed that I needed strength and quickness. That ultimately became our focus.

My youngest brother Phillip graduated from Fairmont that summer. Because he was also a first-rate athlete, Coach Lomax presented him with the opportunity to come to Fort Valley. Phillip accepted and soon became a contributing member of the football team. Now my two brothers and I were attending the same college. Life was good.

★

In September 1966 (my junior year), my athletic aptitude brought me to a significant place. On the court, I was performing in high double figures in scoring and rebounds. Professional scouts began talking with Coach Lomax about my abilities on the basketball court.

I loved playing the game above the rim.

One of the most intriguing scouts was from the Cincinnati Royals, ancestors of the Sacramento Kings. He asked if I'd be interested in leaving college my junior year and trying out for their team. Since my main goal was to become a professional basketball player, I told them "It would be an honor to play for the Royals. However, I made a commitment to several important people in my life that I wouldn't leave college under any circumstances until I received my degree." The Royals congratulated me for making that decision and for keeping my commitment. Nevertheless, they left the door open for me to try out after graduation. What a feeling that was! It was like a dream come true. After that, I just knew I was headed for the NBA.

Fort Valley had a few graduates who were given the opportunity to play professional sports. Two football players quickly come to mind. The Washington Redskins signed quarterback David Bowden from Tampa, Florida, who ended up as a defensive back for a few years. The other was fullback Allen Smith from Atlanta. Allen was so good that everyone knew he had a great chance to make the pros. He was drafted by the Buffalo Bills and played several years. At that time, Fort Valley had never had a basketball player to go to the NBA. I was hoping to be the first.

Also during my junior year, I met a girl named Andrea. She was a senior a Fort Valley—a year older than I was—and I adored her. Something told me that we were destined to be together. Besides working in the cafeteria, I began cutting hair to earn additional money for an engagement ring.

★

Times were tough at the mill that summer so when I moved home I worked at a dry cleaner. There was nothing glamorous about it.

Walking the mile home after a long shift one day I was hot, tired, and sweaty. I approached the house with some clothes slung over my shoulder. As usual, the porch was crowded. I was aware of a man sitting on the swing between mother and grandmother. The man resembled Lamar, but I really didn't pay that much attention. Stepping inside the front door something hit me. *The man looked like my brother but he was older.* Mom called me back outside.

While my eyes focused on this man, I heard my mother's voice saying, "Larry, I want you to meet your father." He remained seated as I walked over to him. We shook hands, exchanged "Hello, how are you's" and that was the extent of our encounter.

Sometime later, I asked mother why he was back from New York and why he had left Griffin in the first place. That's when I discovered that some subjects in life aren't open for discussion. Since this directive came from my mother, I had no choice but to honor it. Later in my life, I learned that my father had another family in Atlanta and his oldest son, Sam Jr., had been shot and killed. My father vowed to stay in Atlanta until he found the person responsible for his son's death.

I'll never understand why he left us. It was the late 1940s and times were ominous in the South. Perhaps he had to leave the city of Griffin. The truth will always remain a mystery to me. Nevertheless, I've never harbored any bitterness or hatred towards my father simply because I never had the chance to know him.

Having caught up on my classes I was looking forward to my last year at Fort Valley. Not knowing what real opportunities awaited me I kept my faith that something good was going to happen. Even if I just graduated from college—what a blessing that would have been! No one in my immediate family had gone to college and graduated. I was driven to be the first.

As I prepared for my senior season, I received yet another Player's Questionnaire Application from the Dallas Cowboys—a budding football team based in Texas. I had been receiving the questionnaires for a couple of years from a man named Gil Brandt, who had the fancy title of Player Personnel Director. Not giving the questionnaires much thought, I completed each one and promptly mailed them back. I figured several athletes received them since they were never accompanied by personal contact.

Also during the fall, I proposed marriage to Andrea and was elated when she accepted my engagement ring. Football season was exceptional and full of personal accomplishments. I was healthy and ready for basketball season to begin. On the court, I continued to average high double figures in both points and rebounds. We had a great team and made it back to the SIAC playoffs.

Teammates called me Goldfingers.

Our last game was on the road against Florida A&M to determine the conference champions. Florida A&M was a strong, physical team and we knew that we were facing the toughest game of the season. Once the game started, it was going in our favor. However, at the end of the third quarter, I went up high above the rim for a rebound and, as I grabbed the basketball, I was pushed from behind. Coming down with the ball, I lost my balance, rolling my ankle as my foot smashed into the court. I suffer a sprained ankle and seriously twisted my knee.

For the first time in my career, I had to be taken out of the game. Boy, did I cry. This game was so important for the school. We were leading before this accident happened but ended up losing the game. That made my pain even worse. I really didn't know how serious my injury was. I just knew it was extremely painful and the ride back to Fort Valley was very long. My right knee and ankle swelled tremendously and I had to use crutches to walk. Through the tears, the only thing on my mind was that my athletic career was over. I had never known pain this excruciating.

Upon arriving back at campus, I was taken directly to the school infirmary for X-rays. Thank God nothing was broken or torn. During my stay, I kept thinking that my basketball career with the Cincinnati Royals was shattered. My teammates would stop by to lift my spirits. I was depressed yet Coach Lomax, once again, didn't seem troubled by my predicament. Even my mother and grandmother didn't appear too concerned. Every conversation ended with "Not to worry, Son," and "Just keep reading your Bible."

After my release from the infirmary, the doctor and trainers prescribed a light exercise program to help regain my strength. My ankle was healing faster than my knee because my knee felt like there was something loose it in. It was still quite painful yet the muscles in my leg were slowly getting stronger.

Shortly thereafter, and for reasons unclear

I was determined to stay in peak physical condition.

to me at the time, Andrea returned my engagement ring and called off our pending marriage. That caused tremendous heartache.

Basketball or Big D?

I've always believed that life is a mystery and still do today. Sometimes the things we desperately want most in life don't always come our way. But as long as we have faith in God and continue to believe in ourselves, doors of opportunity will open. There is a reason and a purpose for everything. As we travel through this world, living the lives we are blessed with, we must be prepared to face any challenge. Sure, we all face hurt and disappointment, but the sun still shines somewhere every day.

My injuries brought me to a very low point and yet I was reminded of the true meaning of life. If you look deep enough *there is a blessing in store for each of us*. Be thankful for what you have. Each obstacle, setback and disappointment takes us to a particular place. There are two choices: stay where you are or move on. One of my coaches always said, "It's not how many times you fall down in life, Larry, it's a matter of how fast you get up."

When my heart finally acknowledged this, life began to change.

★

While lying in my dorm room a few weeks later, still recovering from the injuries and running late for class, something totally unexpected happened. I received a phone call from a gentleman asking, "Is this Larry Rayfield Wright?" (This was amusing because I had never in my life been called by my full name.)

I replied "Yes, Sir! I'm Larry Rayfield Wright. What can I do for you?"

Gil Brandt, Director of Player Personnel.
Photo courtesy of the Dallas Cowboys.

"Larry, my name's Gil Brandt, the director of player personnel for the Dallas Cowboys." (I immediately knew that *this* was the guy who had been sending me those questionnaire applications.) He went on to say, "The Dallas Cowboys are interested in drafting you in the upcoming professional football draft. We're interested in having you play for our football team, Larry."

I was totally taken aback and didn't know what to say. So I said nothing. While collecting my thoughts, I heard Mr. Brandt say, "Hello? Larry? Are you still there?"

"Yes, sir. I'm here." However, since I didn't truly believe it was actually him, coupled with the fact that I didn't know what to say and was late for class, I added, "Sir, may I have your phone number? You see, I'm late for a class and I will have to call you back." So Mr. Brandt gave me his number, stated that he would wait for my call, and that I must call him as soon as possible.

On my way to class, a thought crossed my mind. Perhaps my teammates were playing tricks on me. They knew of my desire to become a professional athlete and they were aware of the questionnaires from the Cowboys. And they knew I had never been contacted by Mr. Brandt.

Even though I had some suspicions, after class I dialed the number and was shocked again when a lady answered the phone, "Good afternoon, Dallas Cowboys. May I help you?" (Well, you've probably figured out by now that when I'm shocked or surprised, I have a tendency to go silent for a moment.) That's exactly what I did.

Again, she said "Hello?"

"Oh…a…may I please speak with Mr. Gil Brandt?"

"Just one moment, please," she said.

When Mr. Brandt answered, I said, "Mr. Brandt, this is Larry Rayfield Wright from Fort Valley State College returning your call."

"Hello Larry. I got the impression earlier that for some reason you didn't believe it was me calling."

"Yes, sir. I thought one of my teammates was playing a trick on me," I confided.

We kind of laughed and talked for a moment. Then he stated, "I'm serious, Larry. The Dallas Cowboys are going to select you in the upcoming draft. We want you to join our football team." At the time, the NFL draft consisted of 17 rounds. He explained the Cowboys' first choice would come in the third round. He also told me that they were going to select me as soon as they could.

"Larry, can you watch the draft on television or listen to it on the radio?"

★

I knew a few things about the Dallas Cowboys. In 1954, Clint Murchison, Jr., a former MIT running back-turned-Dallas millionaire tried to buy the San Francisco 49ers and move them to Dallas. When the deal fell through, he inquired about the Washington Redskins and the Chicago Cardinals, but to no avail. In 1959, the NFL decided to add two new franchises to the league, and Mr.

Murchison was ready to buy. On January 28, 1960, the NFL awarded a franchise to a group of Dallas investors, including Murchison, for $600,000.

The NFL had a policy at the time where only one city could acquire an NFL franchise. Dallas already had an AFL team called the Dallas Texans—owned by Lamar Hunt. Yet, despite the team's success on the field, the club struggled economically. In 1963, the franchise moved to Kansas City and was later renamed the Chiefs.

Mr. Murchison hired Tex Schramm as his general manager, and they immediately went after New York Giants defensive coordinator Tom Landry to be the Cowboys' first head coach. Murchison's hands-off attitude was simple: "hire the best possible people you can find to run your business, then step back and let them run it. And unless you have evidence they aren't getting the job done, leave them alone."

The Cowboys were a young, inexperienced team when they began in 1960. Granted, Coach Landry and Mr. Schramm had an awful pool of players to choose from that year. They were focused on finding bodies to fill each position on the team. Needless to say, their first season was a disaster—1 tie and 11 losses.

★

I had immense respect for Wyomia Tyus' talent.

I also knew that in 1965 the Cowboys drafted Bob Hayes from Florida A&M. Nicknamed "Bullet," Bob was a sprinter who I watched compete in numerous track events. He fascinated me! He participated in the 1964

Summer Olympics in Tokyo along with my high school classmate Wyomia Tyus. Wyomia left Griffin to attend Tennessee State and, at the age of 19, became the first female to win a gold medal in the 100 meters. Bob tied the world record in the men's 100 meters with the time of 10.05 seconds and anchored the gold medal in the 400 meter relay in a record-setting 39.06 seconds. Bob then joined the Cowboys as a wide receiver and kick off/punt returner.

My thought was *the Cowboys drafted Bob Hayes, and now they want to draft me.* Wow! What an incredible feeling.

News about my draft to the Cowboys spread through Fort Valley and Griffin like a pat of butter on a hot roll. I was going to play professional football. Friends and family never considered this a possibility.

The 1967 NFL draft was a week away and excitement was in the air on campus. There was encouragement everywhere, which made me feel good about my accomplishments and myself. Even though I didn't know exactly what was going to happen, I thanked the coaches, teachers and students for their generous support and encouraging words.

When draft day arrived, I was so excited that I actually cut my classes—a rarity for me. I didn't know if I wanted to watch it on TV in the student center or listen on the radio in my dorm room (we obviously didn't have a TV in our room). Xavier Victor, my roommate, wasn't much of an athlete but he was a huge sports fan and a great student. We initially decided to listen to the draft on the radio in our room. Then we decided to watch the draft in the student center where most of the athletes, students and instructors had congregated. After a few anxious moments at the center, I returned to my dorm room with my best friends, Sonny Hillsman and Melvin Johnson. We gathered around the radio with Xavier and wondered when my name would be called. We decided that, given 17 rounds to choose from, it would be after the tenth round.

Mr. Brandt was right when he said the Cowboys didn't have a pick until the third round. We were listening so intently during the third round that one could have heard a pin drop in our tiny room. The Cowboys selected Phil Clark, a defensive back from Northwestern. In the fourth round, Curtis Marker, an offensive lineman from Northern Michigan was selected. Dallas didn't have a fifth round choice, but Sims Stokes, a fast receiver from Northern Colorado, was picked in the sixth round.

Anticipation was building. During the seventh-round, complete silence filled the room. All of the sudden, over the radio, I heard the announcer say, "The Dallas Cowboys have selected Larry Rayfield Wright, a tight end from Fort Valley State College." Those words astounded me. My friends in the room begin to yell. There was upheaval throughout the entire campus.

My pulse was surging as I left the room and sprinted on a sprained knee toward the athletic department. Coach Lomax and the entire staff awaited my arrival. A call from Gil Brandt interrupted the smiles and congratulations. He said, "I just called your dorm, Larry, and they said I could reach you here."

"Yes, sir! I'm here." was my breathless reply.

He continued saying, "Congratulations, Larry. We want you on the next flight to Dallas. Is that OK?"

"Sir, can you please hold on just a moment?"

"Well, yes I can."

Placing my hand over the phone, I told Coach Lomax what Mr. Brandt wanted me to do. "Can you fly to Dallas with me, Coach?"

"Yes, Larry, it would be an honor for me to travel to Dallas with you."

Once I finalized the flight arrangements with Mr. Brandt, I thanked my God in a silent prayer.

★

Coach Lomax and I made immediate plans to fly to Dallas the next day. My excitement over the draft, coupled with my anxiety about flying for the first time, had me over the edge. The itinerary was to drive to Macon and catch a small prop plane to Atlanta. Now, this was my first time *ever* to fly in a plane. I was nervous about that, and, as if that weren't enough, there were torrential thunderstorms in the area. The drive to Macon was difficult in that kind of weather, which further increased my anxiety about flying.

I knew Coach Lomax had flown before and that provided some comfort, yet the plane was small and the weather was absolutely horrendous! We flew through lightning, thunder, high winds and rain. It was truly frightening. Needless to say, prayers were prayed. In Atlanta, we boarded a Delta Airlines jet, a much larger plane with ample legroom.

My knee still wasn't 100 percent, and I remember telling Coach Lomax on the plane, "I sure hope the Cowboys don't want me to work out or do anything physical." He told me he didn't think they would. I didn't know what was going to happen in Dallas. I just knew that this was a tremendous opportunity and I had to take full advantage of it.

An hour and a half after leaving Atlanta, we heard the pilot announce, "Please fasten your seatbelts as we are approaching the Dallas airport. We should be landing in about 20 minutes." Our landing approach took us directly over downtown Dallas. I will never forget my first glimpse of the city. It didn't appear to be as large as Atlanta, but it was definitely bigger than Griffin or Fort Valley.

In 1967, D/FW International Airport didn't exist. The initial phase of construction began in 1969, so we landed at Love Field, the largest airport in Dallas at the time. Gil Brandt and several members of the media met our flight. There were lights and cameras flashing everywhere! They began asking several questions such as, "How was the flight?" to "What does it feel like being drafted by the Cowboys?" I had never been faced with a situation like this. It wasn't about Coach Lomax—I was the center of attention.

After claiming our luggage, we walked to Mr. Brandt's car. It was a new Pontiac—this was probably the first brand new car I had ever ridden in. We headed to the Hilton Hotel, located one block from the Cowboys headquarters on Central Expressway. I had heard of people receiving the red-carpet treatment, but I never expected this would happen to me. After all, I was a 20-year-old boy from the country. Coach Lomax appeared to be calm and collected, so I began to follow his lead. Not having a father in my life to teach me such mannerisms, it was a blessing to have him by my side.

★

Mr. Brandt did a great job in promoting our arrival. At the hotel, we once again were met by a throng of reporters who asked more of the same questions. Mr. Brandt handed Coach Lomax and I keys to two separate rooms. He said to get settled in your rooms and relax for a moment. He would be back in a couple of hours to take us to dinner.

I had never been in such a luxurious place as a Hilton Hotel, and this one happened to be one of Dallas' finest. We had adjoining rooms with a connecting door, and these rooms were certainly larger than any dorm rooms at Fort Valley! There was a king-size bed and a spectacular view of downtown Dallas from the window.

Coach Lomax sat with me while I asked him if he had any thoughts as to what our itinerary would be for the next couple of days. He told me "not to worry," and reassured me that everything would work out. He asked what I thought about my first plane ride. "It was great except from Macon to Atlanta!" I replied. We agreed that the treatment from the Delta flight attendant was befitting of our first-class seats.

After our talk, I slept for maybe an hour. Then Mr. Brandt called, requesting our presence in the lobby in 30 minutes.

We dined that evening in the hotel dining room, and I will never forget that meal. I was told to order whatever I wanted, so I requested a large prime rib with all the trimmings. You hear about how things are bigger in Texas, and this prime rib certainly lived up to that legend.

We talked about where I grew up, my high school days as a student-athlete, my college career and about my plans. Mr. Brandt told us about the Cowboys organization, about some of the players and of their expectations. We talked of leaders on the offense such as Don Meredith, Don Perkins and Ralph Neely. And he spoke of the defensive talents of Lee Roy Jordan, Bob Lilly, Mel Renfro and Cornell Green. It was an impressive and exciting conversation—especially their plans for the future. Mr. Brandt felt that I could play a role in the team's development. Though I played tight end, he indicated that I might play other positions—but first I "had to make the team."

★

Plans called for us to spend the entire next day visiting the Cowboys office and facilities. There we would visit with Coach Landry, Tex Schramm and millionaire Clint Murchison, the team's owner—all of whom were "great men to work for," Mr. Brandt said. I could only imagine what it would be like talking with a millionaire! I could scarcely contain my enthusiasm.

The Cowboys already were my favorite NFL team, mainly because of Bob Hayes, again, who I knew from the SIAC. As a wide receiver, his speed and ability to catch the football changed the way defensive backs played the game. The Cowboys had become an exciting team to watch in their six years in the NFL. They were starting to be competitive on a consistent basis, and the prevailing attitude throughout the organization was that the game of football was about one thing: *winning.* And now I had the opportunity to play for them.

Bob Hayes was an amazing athlete.

It was getting late and, since we had to get up early the next morning, we thanked Mr. Brandt for dinner and said goodnight. When I returned to my room, I called my mother and grandmother and told them everything was going fine, and that the next day would be a busy one. Before saying goodnight, we prayed together.

So much had happened since leaving Fort Valley. Sleep was hard to come by because of the many thoughts running rapidly through my head. Thoughts of mother and grandmother struggling to raise us in a world that wasn't always fair. Now I was finally blessed with an opportunity to make a difference. It was after 3 a.m. before I could sleep.

★

The telephone rang at 7 a.m. It was Coach Lomax saying, "Larry, it's time to get up and get ready. Today will be a long one." With only four hours of sleep, I was still feeling a bit overwhelmed.

For some reason, I considered the possibility of Mr. Brandt offering me an official contract. On our way to the dining room for breakfast, I asked Coach Lomax if he thought the Cowboys would discuss a contract today. He said "Yes, Larry, there is a good chance they might discuss a contract today."

"Coach, you know my situation. If there is one person to speak on my behalf, it's you. You've been like a father to me and, regardless of what happens today, I will forever admire the man that you are and the role you've played in my life," I confessed. This was a touching moment between us. It was a good thing we were the only two people in the elevator.

Coach Lomax, a true man of valor, instilled courage and determination in all of his athletes.

★

During breakfast, we continued talking about my family and growing up in Griffin. When Mr. Brandt inquired about the people who were instrumental in my life, I told him of Reverend Stinson, my Scoutmaster—

and certainly Coach Lomax. Being fatherless, these men encouraged me and gave me guidance.

He asked what my initial thoughts were when I received the first questionnaire from the Cowboys. I

Voted most versatile athlete at Fort Valley.

responded, "Quite frankly, I didn't think much about it. I was a sophomore in college and was focused on playing basketball." He seemed to appreciate my honesty.

"How did you discover me and why are the Cowboys interested in me when no other pro football franchise has shown any interest in me?" was my first question to him.

He answered, "You're a great athlete, Larry, and you have the kind of wholesome attitude we're searching for."

"Since we're being honest here, Mr. Brandt, I must ask this question: Are my football credentials impressive enough to be recruited by the Dallas Cowboys?" I bravely asked.

"This may surprise you, Larry, but the Cowboys aren't necessarily looking for football players," he replied. "We're looking for *athletes* to fit into our system."

"Let me get this straight. You're saying that someone can be a great football player but not a great athlete?" I questioned.

"That's correct," Mr. Brandt explained. "You see, Coach Landry has a master plan, a blueprint for building a solid team. This system needs athletes like you who are adaptable, flexible. Among other things, you can run, punt, catch and play basketball. That's the type of athletic talent that will help us build our team."

He went on to describe the Cowboys scouting system as having several scouts all over the country searching for great athletes. Some were high school coaches, college coaches, even businessmen. A college coach from Florida A&M named Al Tatum directed the Cowboys attention my way. I wasn't familiar with Mr. Tatum but you can imagine my surprise when I learned that he was one of the scouts who discovered Bob Hayes!

Few players are aware of scouts unless they approach an athlete and initiate conversation. The Cowboys had such a thorough scouting system they knew almost everything about me, the different sports I played, all the positions I played in both football and basketball, the fact that I maintained my grades and passed my classes. It was amazing.

"Your size, mobility, speed and ability to excel in two sports captured our attention, Larry," Mr. Brandt said. "The fact is, most athletes participate in just one sport. Others have the ability to *play* more than one sport and more than one position. They haven't accomplished that—but you have."

Hearing those words made me feel as though I was taking my first step into the Cowboys organization. "What position will I play, Mr. Brandt?" I asked. He replied, "Well, we want to test you at several positions, including defensive end and tight end. Coach Landry will make the final decision."

At the Cowboys' offices, it appeared as though the entire staff was awaiting our arrival. Their excitement made us feel as though we had been part of the franchise for years. However, I noticed almost immediately that there were no blacks in the organization. By no means was this a negative feeling—it was just an observation. On occasion, I had been in the presence of whites and was always comfortable with the environment. Moreover, I always cherished my experience with the Cummings family. This was just my first experience in a corporate setting where Coach Lomax and I were the only blacks present. It's very easy to adapt to an environment when people are kind and compassionate.

Coach Landry always brought out the best in others.

Change is not to be feared. Many people fear change because of unknown factors. Personally, I feel that the ability to acclimate to situations and environments is the substance of growth and development. My high school history class, and lessons from my mother and grandmother, taught me that this world is a big place. There are over six billion people on the face of this great earth—people of all nationalities, races, color and creed. People of color account for more than 75 percent of the world's population. By being honest and truthful in treating people the way you would like to be treated is the key to getting along with others. Sadly enough, even people of the same nationality experience problems in co-existing. That day at Cowboys headquarters, I was thankful for my upbringing and my heart was at peace.

After meeting most of the assistant coaches and members of the organizational staff, it was time to meet Coach Landry. A kind and gentle man, he welcomed me to Dallas and invited us into his office. My first look into his eyes was an acknowledgement that this man was a *person of faith*. His presence was captivating. He was special.

Toward the end of our conversation, he mentioned that the new players were coming to Dallas in a couple of months for a weekend workout. What a relief! My knee was still sore and swollen from the injury, and I knew that two more months of rehab would give me sufficient time to heal.

Our next stop was a meeting with Tex Schramm, who directed the team's daily operations. A native of Los Angeles, Tex earned a journalism degree from the University of Texas. In 1947, he joined the Los Angeles Rams as a publicity director. During his 10-year tenure, he rose from publicity director, to assistant to the president, to general manager. Schramm is regarded as one of the greatest innovators in pro football history. Although he didn't coin the phrase *America's Team*, he knew how to capitalize on it. After

Tex Schramm was a shrewd businessman.

a quick introduction, he graciously welcomed Coach Lomax and me, saying, "If there is anything I can do to make your stay better, please let me know. You're in good hands with Mr. Brandt."

We proceeded to the practice field, which, at the time, was located behind the corporate offices. The first person I met was Otis Jackson. A black man known as "Big O," he kept the practice field in great condition and the locker room clean and neat. He was a good man. I didn't know that we were destined to become good friends and share many triumphs and tragedies over the next several years. *Thank you, Big O, wherever you are. May God bless you my friend.*

The locker room was enormous. Players had their name above the locker and their equipment was neatly stored. The trainer was busy preparing off-season workouts for injured players. The rehab equipment for these injured players was certainly different from what we had at Fort Valley.

★

Mr. Brandt had our visit well organized. We left the practice facilities and returned to the hotel for lunch. Afterward, it was back to headquarters for a visit in Mr. Brandt's office. It was time to discuss the contract. Having Coach Lomax with me was comforting because I had no idea what would be fair. I only knew one thing. I wanted to be able to take care of my mother and grandmother. At whatever cost.

Initially I thought $1,000 was a lot of money! It would take someone like me a long time to make that much. With the economy being what it was in 1967, $1,000 would go a long way. The same was even true about $100. I immediately had to adjust my thinking about money and what I didn't have.

With Coach Lomax's assistance, we negotiated what appeared to be some attractive numbers. Mr. Brandt seemed to empathize with our statements and concerns. We thought a two-year contract was fitting while Mr. Brandt suggested a three-year deal.

So we talked about a three-year contract. Recalling Coach Landry said it would take time to learn and become accustomed to his system and to the NFL in general, I realized that three years would give me time to study the system and adjust to life in the NFL.

I remained quiet during the conversation as Mr. Brandt and Coach Lomax began talking dollars. In the end, these were the terms: My base salary the first year was $15,000, a second-year salary of $18,000, and my third-year salary would be $22,000. Silently, I calculated the total dollars to be $55,000! My pulse was pounding but I somehow maintained composure. My heart kept saying "Thank you, Jesus. Thank you, Jesus."

In addition to each contract year, there was mention of a fancy word called "incentives." This simply meant I would receive additional dollars for performances in certain areas, such as becoming a starter, being voted Rookie of the Year, selected to the All-Pro team, and playing in the Pro Bowl at the end of each season.

I quickly concluded that, as a new player and with the starting players, it may be difficult for me to earn incentives. This didn't concern me, but they certainly were nice to have included in the contract.

The best news was yet to come. After talking about incentives, Mr. Brandt said the Cowboys were willing to give me a signing bonus of $10,000. All I had to do was agree to the terms and conditions of the contract. I had heard of players from around the country receiving signing bonuses, but I just looked at Coach Lomax in disbelief. I hadn't played a down nor made the team and they were going to send me home with 10 grand in my pocket!

Then the thought of having my own car suddenly hit me. There must have been a giant question mark above my head because Mr. Brandt asked, "Larry, is there anything else?" Collecting my brave thoughts, I asked, "Sir, since I don't have a car I was wondering if something could be worked out for me to get one?" He asked, "What kind of car are you thinking about?" I told him it didn't really matter as long as it was a good car. "Will a Pontiac be suitable, Larry?" he asked. I replied, "Yes, sir. It would."

So he stated in the contract that I would receive a new car. "Is there anything else, Larry?" I told Mr. Brandt that I would like to see Coach Lomax *taken care of* for coming with me. Then he added "OK. Is there anything else?" I said, "No, sir. That's all." Mr. Brandt called his secretary and asked her to draw up the contract from his notes and have it delivered to Mr. Schramm for his approval.

After about an hour, Mr. Brandt and Mr. Schramm returned with the contract and, shaking my hand, said "Congratulations, Larry. You are officially a Dallas Cowboy."

Pains, Gains & an Automobile

In just a few short hours, I had signed a series of contracts to play football for the Dallas Cowboys, there was a check for $10,000 in my pocket, Coach Lomax was taken care of, and we were on our way to Van Winkle Pontiac to get a new car. It was unbelievable how my entire life had just changed course.

When we reached the dealership, we found the staff was eagerly awaiting our arrival. We were welcomed and sent to the sales office to look through brochures. I selected a Pontiac Bonneville. From the pictures, it appeared large and looked really neat. I chose a gold one with a black vinyl top, black leather interior and a special stereo system that came with a state-of-the-art, built-in eight-track tape deck. Coach Lomax smiled as I selected these features.

This particular car wasn't available on the lot so they had it special-ordered from the manufacturer. It would take about 30 days for the car to be delivered. Arrangements were made to ship it by train to Macon, Georgia. Words can't express the joy that drifted through my body and how thankful I was for this tremendous

blessing. Not just for me but for my family, too.

★

The Cowboys called a news conference for that afternoon at the Hilton to officially announce the signing of their seventh-round draft choice, Larry Rayfield Wright from Fort Valley State College, to a three-year contract. The amount of the contract was undisclosed. Once again, the Dallas media outlets were there in full force. Coach Lomax, Coach Landry and Gil Brandt were by my side. After the conference, things finally began slowing down a bit. We had accomplished our goals and the Cowboys had accomplished theirs.

The last night of this trip was another restless one as I spent most of the time on a swollen knee praying and giving thanks to God.

★

The next morning we packed our bags and headed for Love Field, with a scheduled stop at Cowboys headquarters for another visit with Coach Landry. He shared some upcoming events, especially the invitation to return in two months for a workout. Although I was drafted as a tight end, he still didn't reveal what position he wanted me to play. At the time I was 6-7 and weighed 220 pounds. Coach Landry told me to gain a little weight and "we will go from there." Shaking his hand, I thanked him again for the opportunity.

On the flight back to Georgia, it seemed like I'd been flying for years. It never crossed my mind that this was only my second plane trip. I gazed out the window at the peaceful, brilliant blue sky to reflect on the blur of recent events.

I remember asking Coach Lomax, "Can you really believe the experience I just went through during the past 48 hours?" He said, "Yes, I can believe it. Things have a way of working themselves out."

"But Coach, three days ago I had just $5 in my pocket!"

"Always remember, Larry, that life is a mystery."

We continued our journey in silence until I asked him what I should do about the opportunity to play with the Royals. He said, "Focus on getting your knee healthy for the Cowboys. By the way, I'm very proud of you, Larry, especially with the way you handled yourself with such class and dignity."

Arriving in Atlanta I cancelled my flight to Macon. I wanted to go to Griffin to see my mother and grandmother before returning to Fort Valley. Coach agreed that it would be wise to take an extra day and spend it with them.

I placed a call to mother telling her I was at the Atlanta airport and that Coach Lomax had agreed to let me come home for a day. We still didn't have a car but mother said to wait at the airport and someone would pick me up in about 45 minutes.

After a while, I looked up and saw David Walker, my Scoutmaster. I just knew he was there to take me home. Arriving at his car, my mother jumped out and embraced me with a kiss. Tears were flowing down our cheeks; it was a pleasant surprise.

On the way to Griffin, my enthusiasm continued as I told them of my journey, especially about my first airplane ride. As we approached our front yard, we saw grandmother sitting on the porch. Mr. Walker congratulated me and said, "If there is anything else I can do for you, just let me know." We thanked him for the ride and his kindness.

Big Mama embraced me with a big hug and a kiss. We stood crying on the porch as I began to share my experience. When I got to the part about the contract and the amount of money I signed for, it seemed to take their breath away. The first words out of their mouths were "Praise the Lord! Thank you, Jesus."

After grandmother finished praying, I reached into my pocket, pulled out the $10,000 bonus check, and handed it to mother. "Mom," I said, "This is the beginning of a new change for our family. Good things are going to happen in the future and we are going to make the best of them—in praise and in thanksgiving." When she read the amount of the bonus check, her knees grew weak.

★

The next day I opened my first bank account, then went to visit Mr. and Mrs. Cummings. "Congratulations, Larry," he said. "We believe you'll do well for yourself, your family and the Cowboys."

"Thank you, sir," I replied. "I want to know if you would consider selling us the house my mother is living in." They looked at one another and smiled, saying, "We would be happy to."

It wasn't a big house, three rooms including a kitchen and just one bathroom—which is probably where I developed my quickness. Whenever something went wrong with the house, Mr. Cummings immediately had it repaired. It was in good condition. The Cummings had a big heart for others and it showed. They sold us the house for $5,000. We discussed the terms of the sale so he could make arrangements. One of the Cummings' sons, whom my mother and grandmother helped raise, was an attorney who drew up the legal papers. They would be ready to sign the next day. We thanked them for their kindness and generosity over the years. As we left their home, I couldn't help noticing the tears glistening in Mrs. Cummings eyes. That was a touching and truthful moment.

The next day the paperwork was signed and we delivered a cashier's check for $5,000. For the first time in our lives, we owned our own home. We also took care of all other outstanding bills. Then it was time for me to return to Fort Valley and finish school. I put $200 in my pocket, which was a lot of money for a college student in 1967. I left the balance in the bank for my mother and grandmother.

★

Returning to Fort Valley was like a homecoming celebration. Unfortunately, in every situation of progress and success, there are those who (for whatever reason) seem to change their attitude. These actions are sad and will always remain a mystery to me. When someone advances in life, *it's a blessing*. Some people thought I wouldn't make the Cowboys because of my basketball skills. They thought I should have held out for a pro basketball contract. Well, yes, I wanted to play basketball but I had this opportunity to play football.

My plan was to attend football camp in July and give it everything I had. If for some reason things didn't work out, I still had the second opportunity in August to attend basketball camp for the Royals. Being blessed with two opportunities didn't go unnoticed. Although I was uncertain which path God wanted me to choose, I knew which way I needed to go. There is a huge difference between wanting something—and needing it.

My immediate focus was to prepare mentally and physically for rookie camp in Dallas while directing my attention to graduating in June. My sights on a basketball career during this crucial time were put on hold.

Each day after class, I headed to the gym. I actually enjoyed this time because I treated it like a ballgame: commit yourself, focus on what you're doing and listen to your coaches. At the end of each game, I was exhausted and excited because I had given the game everything I had—and then some. After working out each day, I achieved the same satisfaction.

Leg strength is vital in any sport, especially football. Football players spend several hours developing the short muscles in their legs, which give them leg drive to sustain blocks after making physical contact with opponents. In basketball, running and track, leg strength is built up in long muscles to enhance flexibility and jumping. Athletes excel when they develop both long and short muscles. I put a lot of faith in Mr. Brandt's words when he said that "One can become a great player but there is a difference in being a great player and qualifying as an exceptional athlete." I wanted to be the best.

Not being able to run at full speed was still a challenge for me. I needed to maintain my flexibility for football and quickness for basketball if I needed that to fall back on. There wasn't much time between the two camps and I needed to be ready. My time was spent developing both sets of muscles.

The Trials of Pre-Training

Once again, the Cowboys made the necessary travel arrangements from Macon to Dallas for rookie camp. Fortunately, the weather was fantastic and the flight was uneventful. And Coach Lomax was dearly missed.

A longtime scout from the Cowboys staff, Red Hickey, met my flight. His name was easy to remember because of his brilliant red hair. He had a list of players and checked names as they arrived. Sims Stokes, a wide receiver from Alabama, was the last to arrive. We were introduced and became instant friends. After receiving our luggage, we proceeded outside where two Greyhound buses were waiting. The first one was full of rookies so Sims and I got on the second bus. It was almost full so we settled in the back where we continued our conversation. We appeared to be the only ones talking on the bus—nobody else said a word.

The bus delivered us to the Holiday Inn on Central Expressway, not far from the Hilton where Coach Lomax and I had previously stayed. At the registration desk, we were paired two players to a room. I asked Sims if he would room with me. He replied, "Sure, why not." Being from the South, we figured we had a lot in common. It was a Friday evening and, once we received our itinerary, we realized it was a full and fast-paced agenda.

Our first event was dinner with Coach Landry, Mr. Brandt and some of the recruiting scouts. This is also where we met all of the players and the staff. After dinner, we were advised to get some sleep because "we were going to need it."

Saturday's meeting began promptly at 9 a.m. Dressed in Cowboy-issued shorts and T-shirts, the atmosphere seemed like we were going into battle for the Army. Coach Landry took the lead at the front of the room. He commanded our undivided attention.

We went over our itinerary again and at that point everyone realized that we had taken the next step. We had become professionals. It was nothing like high school or college.

Our next assignment was to hit the practice field for a two-lap run followed by calisthenics. The practice field was marked off with chalk for us to run and be timed in the 40-yard dash. We were paired according to the position we were to play. Thank God I wasn't paired off with Sims. He wasn't nearly as fast as Bob Hayes but he was still incredibly fast! As it turned out, Sims was undoubtedly the fastest player on the field that day.

Through my diligent research of the Cowboys, I knew Coach Landry wanted to open up his passing game by including the tight end in routes designed to put more pressure on the defense. The tight end had to be someone who could block in the running game, run pass routes and catch the football. I was paired with Austin Denney, a tight end from Tennessee. Austin was drafted in 1966 in the 11th round. Although I was a seventh-round pick, it was little consolation because I had overheard scouts talking about Austin and their aspirations of him challenging Pettis Norman, a tough veteran tight end from Johnson C. Smith.

To win a place on the Cowboy's roster I had to perform at my peak so the coaches recognized that I could improve their team. My desire was *deeply rooted*. Whether facing a drill, making a block or taking a lap around the track, I gave everything

The great Mel Renfro sprints as Gil Brandt (kneeling) and other staff members time him.

my all. This was first and foremost in my mind when it came to running the 40-yard dash. I had never run against nor played alongside a white player but regardless of my opponent's race, I was determined to win. Even though my knee was not 100 percent, my desire to succeed was unwavering.

Mr. Brandt and the other scouts were positioned at the finish line, writing down the dash times. I watched each set of players run the 40 yards. Sims ran before me and easily won his race. With the players huddled around the finish line, Austin and I were signaled to start. As we competitively sprinted the first 20 yards, I could hear cheers from the other players. I hit the finish line ahead of Austin by a good three steps. As I was trying to catch my breath, Sims grabbed me and said, "Great race, Larry!" We knew I had won and were curious about my time.

We went to Austin and congratulated him on a great race. He replied the same to me. Sims and I then went to Mr. Brandt to inquire about my time. He said, "For someone your size, Larry, that sure was a great race!" At 6–7 and weighing 225 pounds, I had run a 4.8. However, glancing at Austin's chart, I saw that one of the scouts had written his time as 4.75 seconds.

Sims and I looked at each other in astonishment but neither of us said a word. Even Austin remained speechless. My initial reaction was to say something about the erroneous time one of the scouts had given to Mr. Brandt. But I thought quickly and didn't say a word. Perhaps it was just a mistake because everyone saw that I had clearly won the race and my time had to be faster. Sims insisted I say something to Mr. Brandt but I never did. I just let it go. I found great satisfaction in Mr. Brandt's words and that was rewarding enough for me.

During the next two days, we faced sessions that entailed agility drills, quickness and speed tests, jumping maneuvers, strength and weightlifting techniques. As a tight end and defensive end, I felt the sessions went well for me. When the activities were over, Sims and I had become friends and were confident with our chances of making the team.

Coach Landry had one more meeting with us where he indicated how pleased he was with the workouts and everyone's willingness to participate. He said the next time we would get together would be in July at training camp in Thousand Oaks, California. The rookies were to be at camp two weeks before the veteran players were due to report.

Before I departed, Coach Landry pulled me aside and said he still wanted me to gain a little more weight.

Heading home, I felt confident about my performance and was eager to report to Coach Lomax. I had the time discrepancy of the 40-yard dash weighing on my mind but I was still energized by my experience. Being able to perform alongside other players from across the country was insightful. I always wanted to execute at the highest level possible. At Fort Valley, there were many great athletes with the ability to play professional sports. They could have made a difference in their lives and the lives of others, had they been given the opportunity.

I was beginning to realize that God had answered my 10-year-old prayer and had given me the opportunity to make a difference. The outcome was up to me.

Back in Atlanta, I boarded a Greyhound bus to Griffin to spend time with my mother and grandmother. From there, I returned to Fort Valley and immediately went to see Coach Lomax.

Before we finished our greetings he said, "Larry, your new car has arrived in Macon and we need to pick it up!" We were both eager to leave, so during our drive I told him about the trip to Dallas. "It was fantastic working out with the other players. Everything was coordinated on such a tight schedule," I exclaimed. When I told him of the time discrepancy in the 40-yard dash, his advice was, "Don't worry about it, Larry. There are more important aspects to football than running a 40-yard dash. Stay focused on the entire puzzle, not just the small pieces."

We talked about the necessary elements I needed to make the Cowboys team. He encouraged me to *do my best at everything no matter how much it hurt and to never complain*. When I told him that Coach Landry wanted me to gain more weight, he suggested I begin a special diet that week. He would work with Mrs. Frambo in the cafeteria to get it started. "Just work hard, Larry, and be in top physical condition," he advised.

★

At the train station, I spotted my new car. Coach Lomax introduced us to the manager and told him that we were there to pick up the car. The manager recognized me from the media coverage, yet he still wanted to see my driver's license, just to make certain. The manager then gave the keys to an employee and we headed toward the car. The employee mistakenly handed the keys to

Riding in style in my new Pontiac Bonneville.

Coach Lomax. "Give those keys to that gentleman," said Coach Lomax as he pointed at me. "This is his car." The employee slowly handed me the keys, commenting, "This is one beautiful automobile." Smiling, I replied, "Thank you, sir."

Coach and I got in to check it out and sat in silence for what seemed to be an eternity. I was elated and wanted to relish the moment. Coach interrupted my moment by saying, "Larry, we need to get back to campus. Are you going to start the car?" I couldn't wait to insert my newly purchased Otis Redding tape into the highly innovative 8-track tape deck. It was cool! Life was good.

Back at Fort Valley, with my brothers Lamar and Phillip, we packed our bags and headed home to Griffin for the weekend. During the twilight hours, we pulled into the driveway to find our mother and grandmother sitting on the porch. They had no idea who was in the car until we got out. They where further astonished to learn that the car was part of my contract from the Cowboys. We hadn't owned a family car since 1950.

In keeping with family tradition, we attended church that Sunday morning. Only this time we didn't walk to church, we rode in style. Following the service, friends and family members joined us at our home for dinner that was complete with fried chicken and collard greens. (I can still smell the aroma.) Reverend Stinson said grace before the meal and our home was embraced in a quiet peacefulness as an abundance of praise and thanksgiving filtered throughout the house. I believe God may have sent a guardian angel to us that day.

Back at school, I focused on my final exams, training and graduation, the latter being my main priority. Not only did I want to *achieve* this high priority in my life, I was determined and committed to graduating. So many young athletes leave school early for the pros, which makes it difficult for them to achieve a proper education. Leaving school early, although quite tempting, wasn't an option in my mind.

I didn't want anyone to think that just because I had signed a professional football contract that I didn't have to continue my studies and finish my coursework. My instructors certainly wouldn't let that happen. Besides, I was one of the top students in my class and wanted to finish that way. After finals were over, I felt like I had done well in all of my classes with the exception of biology. Luckily, when the grades were posted, I had passed all of my classes, even biology.

During finals week, I received a letter from Coach Landry expressing how much the organization enjoyed meeting me and how excited they were about my football abilities. He stated that "The observations from the assistant coaches were exceptional." They recommended certain areas of conditioning to concentrate on during the next two months. The coaching staff agreed that by placing me in the best position possible and assigning the appropriate weight class, my chances of making the team would be increased. Their thoughts intrigued me.

Ernie Stautner, the defensive line coach, believed that I had the height and could be a strong defensive force if I were 30 to 40 pounds heavier. To play tight end I only needed to gain another 20 pounds. I was willing to do whatever it took to make the team. Cowboy's trainer Don Cochran sent me a brochure that had several weightlifting exercises designed to help me gain strength.

Coach Landry mentioned that the rookies were given every possible opportunity to make the team. Everyone knew that if a rookie could perform well enough to win his position over a veteran player, it would improve the team. Coach Landry ended his letter by adding, "Football is a very physical game and takes hard work, dedication, commitment, sacrifice, concentration and follow through for a player to become successful."

Thanks in part to Coach Lomax, I felt as though those qualities were already instilled in my heart.

★

A diploma is priceless.

Graduation day was a milestone for the Wright family. Given the extracurricular activities that commanded most of my time, the family was most proud that I had achieved a degree in Education in just three and one half years. And, unlike my high school graduation, this time I was able to buy my own cap and gown. That fact alone was rewarding.

Before leaving the campus of Fort Valley State one final time, I took a sentimental stroll through campus. I reflected on the memories of wonderful students, friends and faculty I had met along the way with the hope of seeing them again one day. Especially those who were among the graduating class of 1967. During my walk, I continued to recite the words of my alma mater *"...Fort Valley State, our lives to thee we dedicate."* I also thanked God for giving this university the necessary tools to grow and develop its students

The two previous trips to Dallas were such a tremendous education and experience for me. I never before had the opportunity to travel. Professional athletes gain national media attention and lots of money and these components can become life-changing events. Couple those extremes with the parties, pretty girls, new cars, fashionable clothes, television and radio interviews, traveling the country; and it was easy for me to see the temptations of fame. Being blessed with my faith and a college diploma gave me the opportunity to prepare for every facet of the future.

My belief has always been *if you start something, finish it and move on.* Do your best and complete the first race before lining up and entering the starting blocks to face another challenge. By doing so, you will never look back with regret. Remember, life is a mystery to live, to love, and to share without hurting others. That's the way I have tried to live my life and will continue doing so until my work here on earth is finished and God brings me home.

Mr. Brandt called a few days later about the Coaches

My college coaches (l-r) Stan Lomax, Alphonso Varner, A. Chester Robinson and James Hawkins.

All-America Game to be played in Atlanta on July 8th. The Cowboys wanted me to play in it. I didn't know how this decision came about and didn't ask any questions—the opportunity was exciting in itself. The competition featured chosen college seniors recently drafted into the league. Some of my teammates included Floyd Little, a running back drafted by the Denver Broncos; linebacker George Webster of the Houston Oilers; and Larry Little, an offensive guard selected by the Miami Dolphins.

My coaches from Fort Valley gave me expert advice on defensive stances and getting off the ball quickly. They also drilled me on pass routes and blocking techniques necessary for a tight end.

It was great competing against players trying to establish a position in the NFL. Playing both tight end and defensive end against the top draft choices lifted my spirits. After the game, I knew in my heart that I could play in the NFL and compete against the pros.

★ ──

This Ain't Boy Scout Camp

It was time to attend Cowboys training camp in Thousand Oaks, California. As usual, the staff made travel arrangements from Atlanta to Los Angeles. Lamar drove me to the airport and I left my new car in his care.

Whenever I imagined California, the Hollywood sign on the hill always came to mind. The few shows I watched on television at the time were *Bonanza* (I'm a fan of Westerns), *The Beverly Hillbillies*, *Batman* and *Mission: Impossible*. Playing at the box office at the time were *The Graduate* (my favorite movie of all time) and *Bonnie & Clyde*.

★

Arriving at LAX, I noticed a man dressed in shorts and a T-shirt holding a sign with my name on it. I approached him and said, "Sir, my name's Larry Wright." He said, "Welcome to California! Follow me and we'll get your luggage." We reached the baggage claim area where there were about 60 guys surrounding the turnstile. They looked like athletes. Shocked, I asked the gentleman, "Are *all these guys* going to the Dallas Cowboys training camp?" He answered, "Yes. Some are second- and third-year players arriving early. Most of them are rookies just like you." The number of players surprised me. I knew the Cowboys drafted 17 players but there were enough guys here to fill out an entire team! When he said that two buses full of players had already left the airport, I didn't have any idea what to expect. I couldn't help but size up the competition as I waited for my bag.

I searched for Sims Stokes but the gentleman said he had left on an earlier bus. So I climbed on board and saw an empty seat next to a player that was as big as he was loud. I asked, "Sir, do you mind if I sit next to the window?" "This must be your first trip to California, huh, rookie?" he asked loud enough for everyone on the bus to hear. "Yes, sir. It is," I replied. His name was Coy Bacon. This was the first of many roads we would travel together.

★

My first impressions of California were unforgettable. I saw literally hundreds of people from all over the world in the airport. Remember, where I grew up people were either black or white. I never had the opportunity to meet or discover other races. And I saw thousands of cars on the freeway and couldn't imagine where everyone was going. Mr. Brandt's words echoed in my mind "Larry, it's a long way from Griffin, Georgia to the NFL." Yes, the road was quite long.

Before leaving college, my friends talked about California girls and how beautiful they were. Well, I had seen pretty girls in Griffin, Fort Valley and especially Atlanta, but in California, they were *everywhere*! Even though they were all different nationalities, their complexions were beautiful, tanned, and healthy—and they looked so happy.

Probably 95 percent of the players on the bus were

20- and 21-year-olds who had never been close to an environment like this before. Everyone was gawking, making comments and laughing. I thought to myself, "This is LA, home of the stars, where dreams come true for so many people. But I didn't realize how many people there were still waiting for an opportunity to make their dreams come true. As the bus left LA, I noticed the Hollywood sign appeared to be as awe-inspiring as it was on television.

★

It took about an hour to get to Thousand Oaks. It was a small city, about the size of Fort Valley. But Thousand Oaks seemed peaceful, and there were mountains—tall mountains—everywhere. You guessed it: I had never seen mountains before.

When we arrived at California Lutheran College, we were sent to the cafeteria to register for camp. The Cowboys had pre-assigned dorm rooms for all the rookies. Sims Stokes and I were assigned to be roommates, along with Levi Davis, a defensive back from Oklahoma. Levi played basketball in college and was almost as tall as I was.

The rooms in the dorms were divided with three beds on one side and three beds on the other. Again, it was almost like being in the Army.

My good friend, Sims Stokes.

Being the first to enter the room, I chose the bed next to the window. Sims selected the one by the door and Levi was left with the bed in the middle. After all, Levi wasn't drafted. He signed as a free agent.

Physical exams were next, and believe me when I say they were *physical* and *thorough*. It was similar to the physical I took for the Air Force. It was amazing how the Cowboys evaluated so many players in such a short amount of time. The elimination process began immediately. Many free agents failed the physical and were promptly handed a plane ticket home or wherever they wanted to go.

Once the physicals were complete, we were sent to the equipment manager who measured each individual from the size of our heads for helmets, to the size of our feet for shoes. Most of us were assigned lockers for our equipment but, because there were so many players, some had to put their equipment on chairs.

From the original 135 rookies, almost 100 remained.

Dinner was next, and to say that "mealtime was strict" was indeed an understatement. We were given a scheduled time to eat and we had to show up. Upon entering the dining room our names had to be checked off a list. The list was then given to our assigned coach to see if anyone had skipped a meal. Even if one decided not to eat, he had to go to the dining room to get his name checked off. If you disobeyed, you were fined for not following the system.

Our after-dinner meetings began promptly at 7 p.m. If anyone came in late or after their name was called, they would be fined. Most of the fines were about $25. Rookies usually didn't have much money since we were paid a *per diem*—a minimal amount set by the league office. In 1967, all NFL players were paid the same amount for training camp. Since I was there to make money, and not give it back to the club, I was early for everything. The evening meetings generally lasted about two hours, and curfew was set at 11 p.m.—meaning we had to be in our rooms with the lights out.

After roll call, Coach Landry would always speak first. At our first meeting, the assistant coaches introduced themselves and explained their expectations for the players in their group. Itineraries were distributed so everyone knew exactly what was going on, where they were supposed to be and at what time they were to be there. I religiously carried my itinerary with me at all times because I didn't want to miss anything or be fined.

Once Coach Landry made his announcements, we separated into three groups. Offensive players went with their coaches and the defensive players went to another room with theirs. Kickers and punters joined the special teams coach. These meetings were strictly business—no joking or fooling around was tolerated. The coaches reviewed plays we were going to work on the next day and advised the players of their position. Many players were assigned positions different from what they had in college. The Cowboys designated positions according to one's athletic ability.

★

Each player received a Dallas Cowboys playbook, which was the size of an entire set of encyclopedias. It was nothing like my college handbook; it was a masterpiece in and of itself. There were literally hundreds of plays and many variations of each play. Thumbing through it, my first thought was "Man! There is no way I'll ever learn all of this." Then it crossed my mind that this is professional football. This is my career, my business, my life. So I dedicated myself, focused and spent all of my extra time learning the system.

The coaches selected certain plays each day for practice. Morning practices were basically spent running those plays, while the evening practices were devoted to passing games and deceptive plays. Deceptive plays were designed to look like they were going one way but really went the opposite direction. They were trick plays designed to fool the defense and they were a blast to run. Each play took patience and execution to work the way it was designed to. It was all about timing.

Naturally, the defensive game is to stop the offense from being successful in running its plays. When the defense changes position two or three times before the ball is snapped, it causes confusion in the blocking assignments of the offensive linemen. Once the offensive lineman is set in his stance, he can't move. If he does, it's a penalty. *Offensive linemen must remain alert and focused on hearing the quarterback's voice.* If the quarterback sees the defense change into another pattern, he can easily change the play originally called in the huddle to another play without anyone moving on the offensive line. This change is called *an audible* and is indicated at the line of scrimmage by calling a certain color or number. When an audible occurs, player's assignments change as different plays are implemented.

So rule No. 1: *It's imperative to be alert and focused on the quarterback's voice.* It's the only voice on the field an offensive lineman should hear. The importance of this lesson was reinforced later in my career. Rule No. 2: Defensive players will do, and say, anything to break the offensive player's concentration. It's called *intimidation.*

Assigned to play tight end, I was used as a blocker and at times as a pass receiver. A tight end must be versatile and resourceful. It was tough enough learning your position but to effectively understand Coach Landry's system, you had to study the other players' assignments. By doing so, you obtained a thorough understanding of what the play was designed to accomplish and why doing your job properly gave you a better chance of making the team.

★

To make certain we understood our roles, each night we were given a written test. I handled this situation as though it were a master's degree, not simply a freshman college course. It was more about technique and execution rather than just blocking and running pass routes. Many players relied on their previous accomplishments instead of learning Coach Landry's system. We actually spent more time in the classroom watching practice sessions and studying films than we did on the practice field. This gave the coaches an opportunity to evaluate the performance of each rookie. Some of the rookies weren't making the adjustments and they were immediately released.

It was apparent why some rookies didn't make the grade but I questioned others. It wasn't necessarily their lack of speed, blocking talents or catching abilities. It was more about their lack of discipline and dedication and being able to adjust to the system. I knew I could handle the physical aspects of playing in the NFL. I had to prepare my mind.

With every free moment, Sims, Levi and I studied our playbook. The assistant coaches presented their report to Coach Landry every night and reported those players who were inadequate. They didn't waste time in sending someone packing. I knew how important discipline was so I respected and followed the rules. Being late for the 11 p.m. curfew was another reason for being released. Unfortunately some players chose to party in LA and violated this rule, quickly prompting their dismissal.

It became obvious when a player was going to be released. He would receive a message that read, "Coach Landry wants to see you in his office and, by the way, bring your playbook to the meeting." This was a strong indication that something bad was going to happen to that player. Sometimes the responsibility was given to the trainer. When players were being taped up before practice the trainers would say, "Coach Landry wants to see you and, by the way, bring your playbook." One immediately knew what was about to happen. With so many rookies in camp, this was a daily occurrence and happened quickly, before and after each practice. It was sometimes hard to remain focused because you didn't know if you were going to be next.

Coy Bacon worked hard and played hard.

To get us through these anxious moments, and throughout our entire training, there was always a comedian who would break the tension and make us smile: Coy Bacon. Coy had played in the Continental League in Canada and, although he never would reveal his actual age, he was older than most of us. We could tell he had been around because of his knowledge of the game. Coy was such a witty guy. When someone would ask him a question, he always replied, "I'm a bitch, boy." Well, we never knew what this meant. I thought he was saying he was a bad dude and don't mess with him. Every time he made the statement we would all laugh. Even the coaches laughed. He was always joking around and cutting up and he never let anything get him down. With practice being so tough, it was great having him around because he was always so happy.

★

On the third day of practice, we faced a scrimmage against rookies from the San Diego Chargers who traveled to Thousand Oaks. We were pumped up because it gave us the opportunity to hit someone besides the players in our camp. It would also give players and coaches from both teams an opportunity to evaluate their players on a different level. The Cowboys had their rookies playing different positions to better evaluate their ability. After the scrimmage was over, I personally thought my performance as a tight end was very good. I caught several passes and made some crucial blocks in the running game. I also played defensive end, rushing the quarterback and making several key tackles.

Along with the coaches, reporters quickly noticed my efforts and I became one of the best prospects in training camp. Several players were mentioned in the sports section of the daily newspapers and every day we would read it to see who was being talked about and what the coaches had to say. The veteran players were one week away from reporting to camp and we realized that they were reading about us and watching television reports back in Dallas. They could easily determine which rookies looked promising and who might have a chance to make the team. That promising rookie just may be the one to challenge them for their starting position. The Cowboys were one of the first teams in the NFL to evaluate players based on their natural athletic abilities instead of just looking at a player based on the position he played in college. By doing this, the Cowboys kept the best athletes available to them to start the regular season. Their concept was to find quality athletes and, if the position he played in college was open, that would be great. But if the position he played in college wasn't available, the coaches would place them in a position that would best help the team. This strategy would also give the rookie the best opportunity to make the team.

Reviewing the rookies are veterans Mike Johnson, Mel Renfro, Cornell Green and Jethro Pugh.

As mentioned earlier, some veteran backup players attended rookie camp. These players made it crystal clear how veterans were going to treat us once they arrived at camp. They shared stories about how the vets would call on certain rookies to run errands for them in the middle of the night, carry their bag, or fetch water. It was also a certainty that we would be singled out after dinner, called to the front of the room and forced to sing our alma mater fight song in front of all the players, reporters and coaches. (I was cool with this because I knew the words to Fort Valley's fight song and was proud of it.) It was amazing, though, how so many players knew every song from all artists on the charts but didn't know their school song. If someone didn't know his school song, he would be asked to sing any song. On the other hand, if a rookie was called to sing and refused to, he had a pretty rough practice the next day.

The second week of rookie camp was almost over and we faced our second scrimmage against the LA Rams. Because it was an away event, we had to dress in our practice equipment, with ankles taped, before we boarded the buses. Other than the helmets and shoulder pads carried in our hands, we were dressed and ready to play football. Time was never wasted.

Our quarterback that day was a dynamic guy named Roger Staubach. He was a promising player from the Naval Academy and the future quarterback for the Cowboys. Drafted in 1964 to take the place of Don Meredith and Craig Morton, he didn't join the team until 1969. Roger spent his leave time from the Navy to attend training camp. After camp was over, Roger returned to the Academy to finish his term.

Roger Staubach as a rookie.
Photo by Bob Lilly.

During this scrimmage, I was selected as the secondary receiver on a certain play. Clearing the line of scrimmage, I noticed the linebacker assigned to cover me was slow getting into pass coverage and I ran right past him. Roger saw me open up as I broke across midfield about 15 yards from the end zone. As I looked back at Roger, he had already thrown the ball to me. It came to me like a speeding bullet.

Reacting quickly, I got my hands up in time to catch the ball, which caused a great deal of pain! I turned toward the goal line and was hit from the side by a defensive back, but didn't go down. I continued toward the goal line. The next thing I knew I was in the end zone. I'll never forget that play because the pain in my hand was from a dislocated middle finger. Roger had thrown the ball *so hard* that the force pushed my finger backward. Initially, I thought it was broken but trainer Don Cochran grabbed it, pulled it back into place, taped it, and put me back in the game. Homer Hill and David Bowden, my quarterbacks in college, could throw the ball hard, but Roger was unbelievable.

I was impressed by Roger's talents. There was something special about him and everyone sensed it. His leadership abilities and attitude about winning football games were commendable. I could easily understand why the Cowboys had such an interest in him. At the time, Don Meredith followed Eddie LeBaron as the starting

David Bowden went on to play for the Redskins.

quarterback, with Craig Morton and Jerry Rhome as the second and third quarterbacks. I hadn't met any of them yet, but we watched them perform in game films during our meetings. Unique in skills and abilities, they were all tremendous quarterbacks. I noticed in the films that they were basically pocket quarterbacks—meaning they didn't move around a lot on the pass plays. Roger was different. He had the ability to run with the football out of the pocket, and he seemed to thoroughly enjoy it.

The rookie squad had been drastically reduced and it was time for the veteran players to report to camp. It was on a Sunday and the coaches gave us the day off, which we desperately needed, although we had to be back for dinner that evening. Most of us took advantage of the off day and went to church. When I returned to campus after church, some of the veterans had already arrived. Some were driving their own cars and others had rented cars from the airport. Most took the bus from the airport, just as we did when we arrived.

I easily recognized some of them from TV and the practice films. It was interesting watching them arrive. Their approach to training camp was nothing like it was when we arrived. We came into camp all quiet and nervous, not knowing what was going to happen or what to expect. These guys were laughing and joking. Some were acting as if they were on vacation.

True to tradition, as soon as the veterans checked into their room they began calling on the rookies to unload luggage from their cars. The vets were the big dogs. The rookies were the fire hydrants. It reminded me of some of the things I went through when I pledged Omega Psi Phi fraternity in college. After church, I went to my room to study for the rest of the afternoon and didn't come out until it was time for dinner. This was the first meeting of the veterans and the rookies. Some of the looks we received made us fearful, but we all had to eat. Most of the players were still in the dinner line when I heard a loud voice saying, "Hey, rookie, get up and sing a song for us!"

There were feelings of embarrassment for all of the rookies called to sing. You had to stand there with your hand over your heart. When my dreaded turn came, I was serious about singing and sang my song with pride. After all, Fort Valley State College provided my brothers and me with the opportunity to further our education. Everyone in the audience realized how proud I was in singing, "...*Fort Valley State, Our Lives to Thee We Dedicate*," and the laughing and joking stopped. Even though I might not have been a great singer, I wanted everyone to know how thankful I was for my education and how much I respected my alma mater. On the other hand, some rookies would get a group together and roll out imitations of the Temptations, James Brown, The Miracles, Sly and the Family Stone or other artists. These moments were such a relief and everyone began looking forward to this part of our day. It also made things easier at practice for the rookies who were favored because of their creative singing.

Still, I remained deeply serious about all the things I did. I was there to make the Cowboys football team and couldn't afford to lose my focus. And when it came time to practice, everyone on the field was getting serious and fiercely competitive.

★

All challenges, whether physical, mental or spiritual, bring out the best qualities in a person in any given situation. Fortunately, through the lessons learned from my mother, grandmother and Coach Lomax, I have always welcomed challenges and learned early on that, to become successful in any of life's endeavors, you must face certain sacrifices. My beliefs, attitude, desire and willingness to learn kept me motivated and strong. A positive, mental attitude was imperative. Now, competing with the big boys, I was ready.

Withstanding all the pain, sacrifices and determination that went along with this very physical sport proved to be a great test of heart and spirit and I never gave up. I remained firmly in the fight. It didn't take the coaches and veterans long to realize this. They recognized that I was there to do my best to make the team and that I could be counted on in tough times and difficult situations.

Our first preseason game was quickly approaching and the coaches would soon select the players who would carry the Cowboys through the 1967 season. The releasing of players was ongoing, with only a few rookies remaining. I was one of them, along with Sims, Levi and Coy. It occurred to us that only a few rookies would make the team. Each NFL team carried 40 active players and retained five players on the *taxi squad* (a fancy term for alternates). So far, the Cowboys had released enough players to build another team. If all teams in the NFL had this type of elimination process, then there were enough players released from each team to start another football league.

After their release, some players continued their football quest in Canada because this was the only option for those who wanted to play professional football. If they didn't choose this path, they went to college or home to seek other employment. My mindset was so focused on becoming a Cowboy that I totally forgot about my other option of playing basketball with the Cincinnati Royals.

Preseason games were established by the league to help finalize the team's 40-man squad, for the coaches and players to get their true timing down on the playing field, and to establish the feel of playing a professional football game. With only four preseason games before regular season, things began to really tighten up. Even though the final roster hadn't been named, I felt as though my chances were good. It was an awesome blessing.

Preparations for this game were nerve-racking for me. Not so much the game itself but the mental part of knowing that millions of people were going to watch on national TV. Just thinking about the folks back in Georgia who might watch the game was exhilarating. I didn't know whether I was going to play but I wanted to make certain that if Coach called my name I would be ready. The coaches had the rookies playing on special teams, which was fine because I played on almost every special team. The Chargers were our opponents and the game was played in San Diego. Everything was just as I imagined it would be with all the fans, cameras and sports reporters. I did get a chance to play tight end and with the kicking unit on special teams. The kicking game is always important because it determines field position. After we won the game, we went back to Thousand Oaks for our last week of training camp.

Once preseason began, we ended our two-a-day practices and everyone was happy about that. These had been the longest practices of my life. As we entered our last week of training, the team count stood at 60 players. Our next game was back in Dallas. During our preparations, most veterans were thinking about being home with their families but the coaches made sure that our concentration level remained high. At this time there was an organization in Dallas called the Salesmanship Club, a group of local Texas businessmen who sponsored the game and gave a large percentage of the funds to an organization to help underprivileged boys and girls. This game was like a homecoming for the team and our excitement escalated. Everyone looked forward to it because of its purpose and for the children who were going to receive financial help. And being our first game of the season played in Dallas, of course we wanted to win.

★

Although we were in our final week of training camp, the veterans never stopped playing games on the rookies. One morning at around 2 a.m., while lying awake in my bed reflecting on everything that had happened in my life over the last six weeks, I saw the door to our dorm room open. We already had our curfews checked so I didn't know what was going on. All of the sudden a large blaze of fire came roaring across the room. It appeared that someone had turned on a blowtorch. Sims was in bed by the door and when he saw the flame of fire shoot across his body he immediately jumped from his bed, dove over Levi's bed, across my bed and right out the window. We knew Sims was quick but we'd never seen such a rapid reaction from him. Then we heard laughter erupting in the

Walt Garrison could heat up more than just the playing field. Photo by Bob Lilly.

hallway from several veteran players. Walt Garrison, one of the veterans, had filled his mouth with lighter fluid, opened the door to our room, struck a match to ignite the fluid, and blew it out of his mouth. It created a long streak of fire that was scary and unbelievable. Needless to say, it was a restless night for the three of us.

Wright On

The remainder of the week was calm and winding down. We packed our bags and boarded the buses to LAX where a Braniff Airlines jet was waiting to take us home. I understood that some of the co-owners of the Cowboys had a stake in the airline, which made sense why it was chartered.

While gazing out the window I reflected on my physical and mental experiences over the previous six weeks. The physical parts were understandable but the mental aspects were something to behold. I quietly asked, *"How could anyone go through so much in such a short period of time and remain sane?"* My mind wandered back to the first telephone call from Gil Brandt expressing an interest in drafting me to play for the Cowboys. Training camp seemed more like six months rather than six weeks. For all the things I had prayed for and wished for as a child,

Training camp was always grueling.

and all the struggles and sacrifices I watched my mother and grandmother endure, it was unfathomable to find myself in this situation.

There were many individuals then and now who are raised in similar and sometimes worse conditions. My prayer is for you to continue with your dreams and keep your vision. Stay in the boat and keep rowing. God will always be there with you, but keep in mind that His job isn't to row the boat. He will bless the work of your hands as you continue to row and He will give you strength to row and will guide you until you've finish the race. No matter where you're from, regardless of your nationality, even if you are not blessed with both parents, keep God in your heart because He called each of us for a divine purpose and He loves you.

While on the plane, I prayed and thanked God for His guidance in my life, for giving me the strength and courage to endure, and for the opportunity to help make a difference in the lives of others. I praised Him for making me the man that I was and for enabling me to pass along what was freely given to me. And I thanked Him for making me the man that my daddy would never become.

Wally, the pilot, interrupted my thoughts by announcing our approach to Love Field. He also mentioned that there was a large group of fans awaiting our arrival. Pulling up to the gate, we could see the fans at the window with banners and posters that read "Welcome Home Cowboys!" Some banners sported the names of players. No rookie names, just veterans. Because of the large turnout, the Dallas Police Department had roped off a path for us but it was hard for them to contain the crowd. Adults and children were asking for pictures and autographs, even from some of us rookies.

The veteran players were allowed to go home but the rookies had to board a bus to the Holiday Inn—our home until preseason was over and the final roster was determined. My new roommate was Coy Bacon.

★

It was a Friday afternoon, two days before the Salesmanship Game. During this era, the Cowboy's home games were played in the Cotton Bowl, which had a seating capacity of approximately 75,000. Children were admitted into the game for $1 and, since the Salesmanship Club sponsored it, we knew that many kids were going to attend. I had never played a game in the presence of so many fans before and, fortunately, we won that game against the Houston Oilers.

It was evident that the coaches were getting serious about what the players were doing on the field, as well as off. It was time for Coach Landry to finalize the team that would go through the 1967 season. After the last preseason game, all of the players were sitting around to see who was going to receive the dreaded telephone call telling them, "Coach Landry would like to see you and, by the way, bring your playbook." We were all on edge.

Unfortunately, Levi had sustained a knee injury, was facing an operation and placed on injured reserve. He automatically became a member of the taxi squad that year. That left me, Sims and Coy. We survived training camp and preseason with only minor injuries. I hurt my knee (the same one I hurt in college) during one of the preseason games but it was going to be OK. We all felt that we had performed well enough to make the team, but we couldn't be certain until we were told.

Finally, word came down from the coaches and none of us had received a call. We were elated. The next morning, the *Dallas Morning News* published a roster of the 1967 Dallas Cowboys. Of the 135 rookies at training camp, only six made the final cut. *Thank God I was one of the six!* Sims made the team as a kickoff return specialist and wide receiver, Coy as a defensive end, and I was a backup tight end.

★

Although Sims was fast and perfect for kickoff returns, the Cowboys had discovered a superstar in Bob

Hayes. As the *fastest human in the world*, his speed as a punt return specialist and wide receiver made him irreplaceable. In order for teams to cover him, they had to change their pass defense from a man-to-man coverage to a zone.

The other three rookies making the 1967 team were Phil Clark as a defensive

It was a long way from Griffin to the NFL.

back, offensive lineman Curtis Marker and Austin Denney, who was eventually traded to Chicago, where he performed well. The veteran tight end was Frank Clarke, who alternated with Pettis Norman. Frank later moved to wide receiver, which opened up tight end positions for Austin and me to back up Pettis Norman, a veteran from Johnson C. Smith, another small Southern college.

Shortly thereafter, a headline appeared in the local newspaper declaring that the six rookies making the 1967 Cowboys were *"Short on Glamour but Long on Mystery."* Looking back on that statement, I understand the writer's thoughts because none of us had overwhelming statistics from our college days and we certainly didn't have much charisma in the eyes of the media. Most of us didn't have a name in the sports world and were drafted from small colleges that didn't get national media attention. But the Cowboys had optimism and confidence that we could develop and help the team win football games.

★

Through the efforts of Gil Brandt, the Cowboys developed a system to reach deep and go beyond the surface of a player to look for athletic talent and natural abilities. This system was inconceivable to many but, at the same time, it opened up a new trend of scouting that brought quality athletes to the game.

By doing so, it brought a mystery to the six selected rookies and a sense of authenticity to the Dallas Cowboy's recruiting system—proving once again that life, indeed, is a mystery.

★

At The Half

It didn't take long for me to realize that life is like a football game. So for your entertainment and inspiration, I would like to share with you some of my revelations:

★ Listen to your coaches. Respect them. Learn from them.

★ Enter each game with courage. Believe that you can win.

★ Face your opponents head on. Learn their every move.

★ Play by the rules. They're golden—and there for a reason.

★ Avoid penalties. They will only set you back.

★ Let your trainers assist you when you fall or become hurt.

★ Treat your teammates with kindness and respect. Support them.

★ If you get called for holding, may you be holding on to what you believe in… or holding the ones you love.

- ★ Listen for the audible. Make certain it's coming from your quarterback and not from the other side of the line.

- ★ Sometimes you'll win. Other times you'll get your butt kicked through the uprights. Keep your chin up and move on.

- ★ If a teammate is called too many times for unsportsmanlike conduct, keep your distance.

- ★ Don't abuse your instant replay privileges. Second thoughts are often regretful.

- ★ Take advantage of your timeouts. Relax. Refocus. Recreate.

- ★ Thank your God—not for making the touchdown—but for giving you the chance and the ability to do so.

- ★ Don't judge a player by the color of their jersey, where they're from, or who their coach is.

- ★ Study your playbook. His written word will be your guidance and salvation.

- ★ Accept your defeats with class and dignity. This alone will make you a winner.

- ★ Acknowledge your friends in the bleachers. Spend time with them. They are there to inspire you.

- ★ If you get called for illegal use of hands, may they be held together in prayer.

- ★ When it's time to retire, do so with grace, dignity and the knowledge that you gave the game everything you had.

- ★ By all means, enjoy your time spent on the playing field. You never know when your number will be called.

Rayfield Wright © 2005

The Second Half

★

Firsts, Fortunes and a Frozen Tundra
1967

Not only was this my first season in the NFL, it was also the first year of the legendary Super Bowl (called the AFL-NFL World Championship Game) where Green Bay conquered the Kansas City Chiefs, 35-10. Wow! Super Bowl I. It's hard to imagine that 39 championships have been played since then.

Some of the first things I did after becoming a Dallas Cowboy were to praise God and call my family. Naturally, they were all ecstatic. Then I set up my finances for the $15,000 from my first-year contract. It would go far in helping many people. I kept some funds to pay my basic expenses in Dallas, a certain amount was sent to my mother and grandmother in Georgia, the balance was invested.

My next priority was to call the Cincinnati Royals to inform them I was declining their offer to play NBA basketball. It was a tough decision—letting go of a childhood dream. Nevertheless, the Royals actually kept the offer on the table for me so if things in Dallas didn't work out, I would still be welcome to play for them. Their acceptance has always been appreciated.

Lamar had gotten married and I knew there was tremendous opportunity for him in a city such as Dallas. In addition, I thought it would be great having him near me. I hinted to him that, since I needed my car and that Dallas was a great place to live with some remarkable universities to attend, perhaps he and his wife should consider moving to Texas. Turns out, they did.

Toward the end of preseason, I had to find a place to live away from the hotel. Most veteran black players

Loving life as a rookie.

lived in south Dallas near the Cotton Bowl where the Cowboys played their home games. The players complained about their apartments being broken into while at practice and on road trips, so I wasn't encouraged by their recommendations. Gil Brandt referred us to a Mr. Dees at the housing authority, who mentioned a new apartment complex in Grand Prairie called St. John's Medallion. Not knowing where Grand Prairie was, Levi, Coy and I drove the 30 minutes west of Dallas along the turnpike, paying our 50 cents each way. Coy and I decided to share a two bedroom while Levi, having just gotten married and expecting a child, settled into a one bedroom.

All of us were so young that we thought it would be cool living out in Grand Prairie and commuting. We left early in the mornings and arrived home late most nights so the travel grew wearisome. Sometimes when we had a day off we would go to the nightclubs in Dallas, but that was never really my scene. I enjoyed dancing and listening to the music, but drinking and partying wasn't a priority for me. Even while in high school and college, I never found the clubs and nightlife very exciting.

★

However, the energy on the playing field was exhilarating. Since the 1966 season ended with a 10-3-1 record and a second consecutive playoff appearance, a spark ignited throughout the organization, the players, the city and the fans. The Dallas Cowboys were serious contenders in the NFL. Very few teams in their seventh year had ever experienced that degree of success, and demands were being made to surpass all expectations. As a rookie, I was driven with a concentrated desire to help my team become successful.

There were also many firsts for the Cowboys that year. They had the vision to reach out and go beyond the surface in selecting players. By doing so, it brought a mystery to the elect and a truth to their convictions. Although their strategy was puzzling to many, it brought a certain eminence to the organization.

Professional football, at this time, was beginning to overtake baseball as the favored team sport in America. The American Football League (AFL) was stocked with more black players and a surplus of free agents and talented athletes with no professional football experience. Remarkable players such as Joe Namath, Lance Alworth, Len Dawson and George Blanda— who would later make history with the most games ever played—were AFL stars. The AFL consisted of the Houston Oilers, New York Jets, Buffalo Bills, Miami Dolphins and Boston Patriots in the East, and the Oakland Raiders, Kansas City Chiefs, San Diego Chargers and Denver Broncos in the West. Compared to the NFL, the AFL was more decorated with flashier uniforms that sported the players' names on their jerseys.

119

The NFL also established a new format where teams were separated into *divisions*. (Divisions and expansion teams were buzzwords in 1967.) With 16 teams in the NFL, four teams were in each division. The **Capitol Division** consisted of the Cowboys, Washington Redskins, Philadelphia Eagles and New Orleans Saints. The **Century Division** included the Cleveland Browns, St. Louis Cardinals, New York Giants and Pittsburgh Steelers. The Capital and Century Divisions formed the Eastern Conference. In the **Central Division**, the teams were the Green Bay Packers, Chicago Bears, Detroit Lions and Minnesota Vikings. The San Francisco 49ers, Baltimore Colts, Los Angeles Rams and Atlanta Falcons joined the **Coastal Division**. The Western Conference consisted of the Central and Coastal Division teams.

This was a remarkable system where each team competed within its division twice each season and the rest of the games were among teams from other divisions. This move brought more rivalry and enthusiasm to the game.

During this season, Cowboys owner Clint Murchison Jr. announced plans to build Texas Stadium—probably because the Cotton Bowl wasn't, shall I say, in the most privileged part of the city. Initially, the new stadium was to be built south of downtown but this arrangement didn't develop, so property was purchased in Irving, a smaller city northwest of Dallas. There was even talk of changing the name to the Irving Cowboys. A quirky name but more fitting than the first one selected—the Dallas Steers. Thank God that name didn't stick around. Could you imagine?

The move to a new stadium caused conflicting emotions for the players, the fans and the city of Dallas.

The Cotton Bowl held 75,000 fans; the new stadium would hold only 65,000. As a child and throughout Boy Scouts, I knew what it was like to be on the receiving end of ones mentorship and generosity. Since children could attend games at the Cotton Bowl for $1, several teammates and I sponsored 100 children to watch each home game. The new stadium called for higher ticket prices, and parking costs alone would run $5 to $10 per game. We soon realized that it wouldn't be feasible for us to afford such extravagant prices, so sponsoring the children would become impossible. This caused me great concern.

★

Whether young or old, black or white, male or female, people from all over the world enjoy sports. I believe that God designed sporting events as a vehicle to break through barriers and perceptions. I remember seeing black athletes such as Jesse Owens, Joe Louis, Wilma Rudolph and Wilt Chamberlain become pioneers in their respective sports. They were blessed with exceptional talents and touched many lives.

During my first few games, it was amazing to witness changes in the lives and hearts of people all over the world. Playing on special teams, I had an occasional opportunity to observe the fans in the stadium. They were from different walks of life joining together for one purpose... *a football game.* Coming from the segregated South, this was my first experience seeing people unite for such a *simple* cause. My wish was for everyone at these events to appreciate the moment and carry this unity home to their families, schools, jobs, and communities. If this type of harmony was practiced every day, what a wonderful world this would be.

★

After easily winning the Capitol Division, we headed for the playoffs for the third consecutive year. In the first round, we demolished the Cleveland Browns by a score

Players enjoying the morning before the Ice Bowl.
Photo by Bob Lilly.

of 52-14 at the Cotton Bowl on Christmas Eve. Before a record crowd of 70,786 fans, Meredith connected on 10 of 12 passes, for 212 yards and two touchdowns. Hayes attained 285 total yards while Perkins crossed the goal line twice. It was the first playoff victory for the Cowboys and gave us the title as the Eastern Conference Champions.

On December 31, we traveled to Wisconsin for a rematch against the two-time defending champion Green Bay Packers. The winner would advance to Super Bowl II. The match-up between coaching legends Vince Lombardi and Tom Landry was newsworthy, but the weather that day was history-in-the-making. Temperature at game time was 13 degrees below zero and the 15 mph winds caused a windchill of *minus 40 degrees*. As the sun left the

stadium, temperatures dropped even further. It was cold. *Bitter cold* doesn't adequately describe the weather that day. Lambeau Field truly was a frozen tundra.

Lambeau Field—the coldest place I've ever been.
Photo by Bob Lilly.

To prevent freezing on the field, an underground heating system was placed six inches underneath the turf. At first, Coach Lombardi refused to let us work out on his field, but he eventually turned back *half* the tarp, which gave us some room for practice. I quickly realized that no weather conditions *whatsoever* would stop an NFL football game. Amazingly enough, the stadium was packed to capacity with 50,861 fans dressed like Eskimos in hunting coats, ski masks and hooded parkas.

Our team tried to dress accordingly but we didn't have the luxury of sideline heaters and thermal socks. Some players wrapped their feet in plastic wrap. One trainer told us we were "sissies" if we chose to wear gloves. Playing on special teams, I spent the day in constant motion on the sidelines to keep the blood flowing throughout my body. Other players huddled on the bench relying on sheer body heat for survival. I recall Bob Hayes running pass routes with his hands stuffed through slits cut into the sides of his jersey. Many players, myself included, still suffer the side effects of frostbitten toes, fingers, even ears. Had the game gone into overtime, some would have suffered even more serious consequences.

Early in the game, Bart Starr kept his cool and connected with Boyd Dowler for two touchdown passes. Down 14-0 in the second quarter, our defense ignored the icy elements and recovered two key fumbles to close the gap 14-10. Coming out of the toasty locker room to face the third quarter, we suffered heartache with a Don Meredith fumble and a missed field-goal attempt. In the fourth quarter, we took a 17-14 lead when Dan Reeves tossed a 50-yard touchdown pass to Lance Rentzel. With 16 seconds left on the game clock, we found the Packers knocking on our one-yard line. Our defense was secluded in the end zone without the benefits of the underground heaters. The solid layer of ice withstood the desperate attempts of our linemen to get the slightest bit of traction at the line of scrimmage.

With precious seconds remaining on the clock, we assumed Starr might roll out to throw or run. However, the quarterback sneak he executed drove him to the right side of his offensive line over the blocking of Jerry Kramer and into the end zone for the 21-17 victory. Regardless of which team had better traction on the playing field or if anyone moved (or was offsides), our spirits were as low as the goal posts the Packer fans twisted down after the game. For me, it was remarkable to play in one of the greatest games in NFL history. A

game literally frozen in time…and in my mind. Yet in spite of the weather, my heart was left numb from the loss and the fact that we came up short, once again, without the NFL title.

Surgery was the last thing on my mind.

After every season, the team doctors checked players for injuries before releasing them for the off-season. I was suffering from torn cartilage in my left knee and was scheduled for immediate surgery at Baylor Hospital in Dallas. I was hesitant about going under anesthesia for the first time, but the support and prayers from my family and friends gave me strength.

My surgery went well and I spent some recovery time back home in Griffin. You know, there are certain times when a mother's home cooking and TLC is the best medicine. The time in Georgia also gave me a chance to see friends from Fort Valley—Dean Brown in particular. As one of my college teammates, Dean was a great athlete who received an invitation to play defensive back with the Cleveland Browns. We had several NFL notes to compare.

Also during this time, Andrea wanted a second chance at a life together, so we began communicating once again. I still loved her and decided that if we felt the same way about each other after the next season, we would eventually get married.

Dean Brown.

My knee operation was successful and I began working diligently on strengthening and conditioning it for the duration of the off-season. It wasn't mandatory to work out at the training facility, but the trainers kept a chart of our program and, since Coach Landry and the coaching staff worked out most days, they knew who was serious about their training and who wasn't. Knowing the coaches wanted players to be in peak physical condition at training camp, I concentrated at being my best.

★

Perk took me under his wing.
Photo by Bob Lilly.

As a rookie, I was fortunate to find a friend and confidant in Don Perkins. Regarded as a player's player, "Perk" was a terrific running back who had played eight seasons. One day he asked, "How many years do you plan on playing football, Larry?" I replied, "As many as I can!" He then told me he was retiring at the end of the season and moving back to New Mexico for a career in politics. Before leaving, he offered some sound advice: "Learn the system. Stay healthy. Listen closely and learn as much as you can, not just about football, but also about how the organization works. Make as much money as you can and invest it wisely. And no matter what happens, Larry, walk away from the game with your head held high."

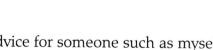

It was powerful advice for someone such as myself who was naïve about the structure of the league. We shook hands with the promise that I would pass this knowledge on to the younger players.

Changes & Challenges
1968

The Cowboys signed solid building blocks in '68 with D.D. Lewis, a linebacker from Mississippi State, defensive tackle (at the time) Blaine Nye from Stanford, and Larry Cole, a defensive end from the University of Hawaii. When Larry Cole's name appeared on the roster, Gil Brandt noticed that there were many players on our team named Larry. (Larry Cole. Larry Stevens. Larry Wright.) To avoid confusion, Gil began calling me Rayfield (my middle name) and I've been attached to the name ever since.

I wasn't a threat for Pettis Norman. Photo by Bob Lilly.

While still sporting No. 85 on my jersey, I continued playing third-string tight end behind Frank Clarke and starter Pettis Norman while my drive to become a starter accelerated. My first year in the NFL was a tempting appetizer. Now I wanted the full meal. I was hungry.

★

The Cowboys offensive and defensive systems weren't standard in the NFL. The offense involved a lot of movement, repetition and total concentration just to comprehend it. All the shifting and movement was designed to confuse our opponents, and we had to know the system to execute it properly. On the field, response had to be automatic. NFL teams needed any edge they could get because players and opponents had elevated their game. I believe the Cowboys were successful during this era because of the dedication and commitment made by the players and coaches in the off-season. In 1968, most teams didn't have strong off-season programs, which became apparent during preseason games because they weren't as conditioned as we were.

The same was true for the defense. Most teams

Lee Roy Jordan was muscle in midfield. Photo by Bob Lilly.

implemented a 4-3 defense where all four defensive linemen were on the line of scrimmage. The innovative *flex defense* was designed to play pass and run with two defensive linemen taking their starting position off the line of scrimmage in a reading position. It was unique and different, but very successful. The flex defense also made it tough for the offensive linemen to get to the middle linebacker, who would roam around in hopes of making a tackle. In my opinion, we had the best middle linebacker in Lee Roy Jordan. He wasn't very big, about 210 pounds, but he was quick and agile. He certainly got the job done and did so by starting 154 consecutive games. The flex was a brilliant concept and it worked with determination and discipline. Coach Landry was the master innovator of our offense and defense.

★

We began the season on a mission—winning our first six games. Our team was dynamic. What football fan doesn't remember Bob Hayes, Don Meredith, Don Perkins, Dan Reeves, Craig Morton, Pettis Norman, Frank Clarke and Walt Garrison? All of them are legends in their own way. The offensive line was the best in the NFL, with tackles Ralph Neely and Tony Liscio, John Niland and Leon Donahue at guard; and Dave Manders at center. Our defense included tackle greats Bob Lilly and Jethro Pugh; George Andrie and Willie Townes as ends, while Lee Roy Jordan, Dave Edwards, Harold Hayes and D.D. Lewis came in as linebackers. Behind the linebackers were Mel Renfro, Mike Gaechter, Herb Adderly and Cornell Green—the first free agent to leave an impression on the Cowboys.

★

During a game against Philadelphia at the Cotton Bowl, Coach Landry sent me in to play tight end. We were on the Eagle's 15-yard line and Meredith called a pass play making Bob Hayes the primary receiver. Bob was well covered, so Don looked to Lance Rentzel, who was also enclosed. My job was to check and hit the opposing linebacker, then release across midfield as a safety valve for the quarterback. (The tight ends in Coach Landry's system were never the primary receiver

Always smiling and singing, Don Meredith. Photo by Bob Lilly.

but rather were used as decoys and blockers—so many

defensive players never paid much attention when they released on a pass route.) Seeing the Eagles' linebacker move away from me to his pass coverage, I released on my pass pattern. When I looked back at Meredith, all I saw was the ball spiraling towards me. I was wide open and Meredith read the defense perfectly. Catching the ball, I was just as surprised as the Eagles defense! Turning toward the goal line, I was hit by a defensive back around the 10-yard line. He clutched my leg as I carried him and another defensive player across the goal line for my first NFL touchdown. It was also my only touchdown that season and a proud moment. Meredith deserved a lot of the credit for that score. He was a great quarterback and technician of the game.

Years later, I asked Don if he remembered that particular pass to me. His quick-witted comeback was, "Hell, Rayfield. I wasn't throwing *you* the ball. You're so damn tall that you just got in the way!"

For the second consecutive year, we won the Capitol Division when we landed a 28-10 victory against the Giants at Yankee Stadium. Yet we failed to win the Eastern Championship when Cleveland defeated us, 31-20. That season we allowed just two rushing touchdowns and scored a league-high 431 points.

The NFL owners added a new dimension to the game when they introduced the Playoff Bowl. Our opponents were the Minnesota Vikings—losers of the Western Championship. We took the game with a score of 17-13 to come in third place. Nevertheless, who wants to be third? Some people called it the Runners-Up Game. We termed it the *Loser Bowl*. Fortunately, this challenge didn't stay in the league very long.

After the season ended, Andrea and I were married in June of '69. With my family taken care of and my knee completely healed, I was a happy young man. Still unsure of what position I would play, I continued praying to God and studying my playbook.

The BIG CAT Unleashed
1969

Each day after practice I traveled south on Central Expressway past Oak Farms Dairy north of downtown. Their facility sported a gigantic billboard saluting the Cowboys "Player of the Week." Imagine my surprise one day when I noticed the billboard read Unleash Rayfield Wright! It was a humbling experience seeing my name so boldly and publicly displayed. Little did I know it was the beginning of a marketing campaign that would encompass the entire country and last for several weeks.

It took some digging but I eventually discovered the catalysts behind the tongue-in-cheek media blitz. They were Charles Breckenridge and Jon Brobst, recent graduates from Texas Tech caught up in the media drama the team was receiving.

Coach Myers looks on while I unleash on the punching bag.

Keep in mind... the Cowboys were newsworthy and any story about any player sold a ton of newspapers. It didn't matter whether a player bought a new tie or got a haircut.

It generated ink.

Anyway, Charles and Jon had researched my athletic background and became intrigued by the mysterious way I entered the organization. They knew I could punt, run, block—do almost anything on the football field—and they wanted to see me do it. At the same time, they wanted to mess with the media.

Therefore, Charles and Jon began abusing their copy machine privileges where they worked and produced thousands of press releases and flyers encouraging fans to *Join the Unleash Rayfield Wright Fan Club*. Every week, they mailed leaflets and press releases to media outlets in North Texas and to national sports magazines. They put up banners in the stadium and posted signs on several local marquees. Their concept caught on like wildfire. The story was hot! Soon they had 40,000 fans signed up into the club and the numbers increased weekly—by the thousands. By preseason, there were nearly 80,000 active fans wanting to see Rayfield Wright *Unleashed!* It was insane and I've always treasured their efforts.

The funny part of this story, which I just recently discovered, is that a few years later Charles went to work for the Cowboys and never told a soul that he helped instigate the Rayfield Wright Fan Club. So why the secret? Perhaps he didn't want to feel the wrath of Tex Schramm unleashed on him? But that's just a guess.

Wright Tackle

During my first years playing tight end, I enjoyed handling the football. I'll never forget the day Coach Landry called me into his office and said, "Rayfield, I want to move you to the offensive line. Because of your willingness to learn and your height and quickness, I believe you could develop into a great offensive lineman." Sitting in stunned silence, I allowed him to continue. "We're rebuilding the offensive line to become a faster, quicker line to accommodate the flexibility of our quarterbacks." Well, that made sense to me.

Coach Landry ended our meeting by saying, "If you gain a little more weight, Rayfield, you might have a chance at becoming a starter as an offensive tackle." *A starter?* That's all I needed to hear. I replied, "Coach Landry, if you believe in me enough to play this new position, having never played it in my entire life, I will give it *absolutely everything* I have." A handshake agreement sealed our conversation.

★

Knowing that I needed to be closer to the training facilities, and since the commute from Grand Prairie was growing tiresome, Andrea and I moved to a house in Oak Cliff, a family community where other players had relocated. Needing to gain another 25 pounds, I met with offensive line coach Jim Myers. He felt that I could carry the extra weight without any problem and wanted me to report to training camp weighing close to 260 pounds.

Commander and Coach Jim Myers. Photo by Bob Lilly.

I also wanted to know everything about my new position, so I asked Coach Myers for access to some game films. He thought that was a great idea and had me meet with Bob Friedman—the keeper of the films. Bob had an assistant named Radar, a helpful black man. (His real name still remains a mystery.) Radar asked, "What films would you like?" Thinking of the best offensive tackles at the time I requested three:

Philadelphia, Green Bay and St. Louis.

Setting up the projector in my study, I scrutinized these films every waking moment. The Eagles had Bob Brown, a big, brawny guy weighing close to 300 pounds. Nicknamed *Boomer*, he had a forearm like an exploding bomb. His stance was wide and he could throw his forearm hard against a defensive player. All of his moves were quick. I also studied Bob Reynolds and Ernie McMillan of the St. Louis Cardinals and the Packers' Forrest Gregg (a nine time Pro Bowl selection who had a brilliant career). They were all physically strong and had exceptional balance.

★

Power-player Jethro Pugh.
Photo by Bob Lilly.

With Jethro *Buzz* Pugh as my roommate, I was back in training camp feeling like a rookie all over again but ready for the ultimate challenge. Upon entering the locker room, my number 85 jersey was replaced with 67. Now, I knew that *the number didn't make the player*, the player made the number. Still, 67 just didn't feel right. It wasn't balanced. Buzz seemed to understand my displeasure.

Nonetheless, I was energized! Looking at some veteran players on the field, I was even more encouraged. There was Cornell Green; a fabulous basketball player from Utah who had never played football yet became one of the best defensive backs in Cowboys history. Pete Gent, another basketball player, was converted to a tight end. Of course, there was Olympic-great Bob Hayes who was instrumental in opening up our passing game as a wide receiver.

It was going to be interesting to see how Coach

Landry would manage the quarterback situation. He knew how to handle challenges and was determined to have a winning team. Craig Morton was our new quarterback and a great athlete. Similar to Meredith, Craig wanted to call his own plays, like most quarterbacks in the NFL, but Coach Landry had other plans. Jerry Rhome was the back-up, followed by Roger Staubach, a 27-year old rookie who'd just completed a four-year hitch in the Navy. Each player was rich in talent, and Coach had a tough decision. Regardless who was behind me on the line, I was going to shelter and protect them.

★

Training camp was going well for me until our first scrimmage against San Francisco. My job was to block Tommy Hart. He was signed at the same time I was from Morris Brown, a small black college in Atlanta. Tommy was strong and quick off the ball. During this scrimmage, Tommy and I were head-to-head on a play where his job was to rush the quarterback. I got into my stance, looking straight at

QB Craig Morton.
Photo by Bob Lilly.

Tommy, when the ball was snapped to Craig Morton. While Craig was setting up in the pocket to throw, Tommy struck me hard, knocked me off balance and literally picked me up and slammed me back into Craig. I landed on Craig. Tommy was on top of me and the ball lay on the ground. The next thing I heard was Craig screaming "Get the hell off of me!" Everyone was laughing and I was completely humiliated. During all of my sporting days, nothing like that had ever happened to me. It was crushing. I may be a big guy but I've never met anyone who isn't sensitive when laughed at or ridiculed. That hurts. Right then and there, I made a commitment to myself. *Whatever it took*, I was going to learn to play that position.

★

Pass blocking is an art. Recalling my brother's advice when I was a young athlete, I soon recognized that I couldn't block like these players in the films. I had to reach deep down inside to discover my own techniques. If I  didn't, my insecurities of thinking *"The Cowboys moved me to this new position because they want to get rid of me,"* would eat me up. Plus, I never wanted to be embarrassed like that again. Since I had always relied on mentors for guidance and knowledge, I went directly to Ralph Neely and Tony Liscio —the offensive tackles for the Cowboys. Their willingness to help me learn and grow was invaluable.

All-Pro Ralph Neely.
Photo by Bob Lilly.

Ralph, whom Dallas acquired in 1965 by sacrificing four top draft choices, was the younger of the two. Although Tony was nearing retirement and had a bad knee that required surgery, he was able to maintain his starting position at left tackle. Always a professional and a team player, Tony recognized that I needed to work on my pass protection and agreed that no two players could block the same way. Offensive players have an advantage because they know exactly when the ball is going to be snapped. Since my greatest asset was quickness, Tony began my lessons each evening after practice concentrating on the quickness in my setup so that I could get into a comfortable position without being off balance.

Initially, I was setting up by taking a step forward. This approach wasn't bad, but I felt overextended and it didn't put me in a very aggressive or balanced position. Then I recalled how basketball training taught me how important it was to shuffle my feet to stay in front of the player with the ball. Once you cross your feet, you're beaten. Therefore, I began to simulate that type of position—shuffling my feet for balance and strength, with the quarterback representing the basketball goal. My job was to keep the defensive ends away from the basket. As long as the quarterback remained where he was supposed

Tony Liscio took time to teach me.
Photo by Bob Lilly.

to *(yeah… right)*, I stood a good chance of keeping the defensive player at bay.

With the double shuffle, my feet remained shoulder-width apart, making this new stance comfortable. At the time, no other offensive lineman in the NFL was using a double shuffle in his setup and it was a good feeling to know that I developed a position that would work for me.

Quarterbacks use several set-up positions depending on the pass play called. This determines the depth in which he will drop back from the line of scrimmage. This is important information for an offensive lineman because it determines the aggressiveness of his blocking. With a short or quick pass, the lineman must be very assertive. On a deep pass play, which takes longer for the receivers to run their pass routes, the quarterback sets up deeper and a pocket is formed with the center and two offensive guards solid up front while the two tackles drive the defensive ends around the quarterback. Whatever it takes, the quarterback needs time and protection.

★

A groundbreaking ceremony for the new stadium took place with Bert Rose as the stadium's general manager. Not only was an era ending for our games at the famed

Bob Hayes changed the game of football.
Photo by Bob Lilly.

Cotton Bowl, but Dandy Don Meredith turned out the lights on his football career and announced his retirement. Don was a pocket quarterback, not a scrambler, so the linemen always knew where he was in order to protect him. He also displayed character, whistling talent and humor on the playing field. Sometimes the coaches would send in a play and, most of the time, he would run it. But since Meredith always had a feel for the game, if he didn't like the play, he would kneel down in the huddle, deep in thought and say, "OK, guys, this is what we're going to do." Most times, his call would work. During one game in particular, he turned to Bob Hayes and said, "Your defender is playing you on the outside so fake him out and take off down the middle of the field. I'm going to lay the ball down the center for you to catch. Linemen, give me three seconds and we'll have a touchdown." After the ball snapped, the play happened just as he called. Given his vast knowledge of the game, I can't help but wonder how many records Meredith would have set had he played longer and with a better offensive line to protect him. He was awesome. Some people say that I caught the last pass of Meredith's career. Honestly, I don't know if that's a true statement.

A month after Don's retirement, at age 31, another prominent career ended for our all-time leading rusher, Don Perkins. These guys helped pave the way for the Cowboys during the early years. I remember how Perkins would carry the ball up and down the field for 100 yards or so and was rarely called upon to score the touchdown. But because he was a team player, he never complained about it. He just wanted the Cowboys to win football games.

"Welcome to the NFL, Rookie!"

We charged out of the chute early in 1969 taking a six-game victory ride. Then the Cleveland Browns, who had ended our previous season, mangled us by a score of 42-10 on their turf. The loss was bitter.

Prior to our game against the Rams, Ralph Neely was injured. The team thought Jim Boeke, because of his experience, would replace Ralph. Instead, Coach Myers called me with the news that I was going to be a starter at right tackle. After thanking God for this blessing, I traded in my number 67 jersey for 70. It was a bolder, more commanding number. (It wasn't until 1973

Balanced, up front and on the line.

when the NFL adopted a standard jersey numbering system. Players who had been in the NFL until then could continue using their old numbers. The following system was implemented: 1-19 for quarterbacks and special team players, 20-49 for defensive backs and running backs, 50-59 for centers & linebackers, 60-79 for defensive and interior offensive linemen (other than centers), 80-89 for tight ends and wide receivers.)

When the media caught wind of my new obligations, reporters began pursuing me for interviews. It took me awhile to realize that it wasn't so much me or my new position they were interested in but about the player I was going to face in my first game. Everyone knew the LA Rams had the Fearsome Foursome led by All-Pro Merlin Olsen, Lamar Lundy and Roosevelt *Rosey* Grier. But I was going to be challenged by the Secretary of Defense himself, David *Deacon* Jones. Players and coaches throughout the NFL feared this ferocious defensive end and shuddered at the thought of having to block him. After all, he didn't earn his nickname by being a nice guy.

I still didn't fully understand what all the fuss was about until I began studying game films on the Rams. Deacon was absolutely ruthless. On pass plays (the calls he seemed to relish the most) he was difficult to block and control and usually made his way in for the sack. Double-teaming him was rarely successful. The league didn't track sacks and hits back then but he probably averaged six to seven sacks per game.

While studying the films, I saw him brutally slam offensive tackles upside the head with a nasty move called

Willie Townes helped me keep my head.
Photo by Bob Lilly.

the *headslap*. He was so quick off the ball that the lineman didn't get a chance to set up. Deacon would headslap them so fast and so hard that sometimes their helmets flew off their head. It finally dawned on me what the big deal was so I continued to study and mentally prepare myself for the challenge.

Teammates Jethro Pugh and Willie Townes worked with me after practice that week, which was a tremendous help in my preparation. The headslap was so devastating that most linemen would duck their heads, leaving them in the dust. Jethro and Willie helped me develop a technique that would prevent me from ducking my head—or from losing it. The NFL had a rule where offensive linemen couldn't extend their arms. We were taught to block by grabbing the fronts of our jerseys. My new method was similar to a boxer's move—block the punch and throw one right back while not extending my arms. It was a rapid, continuous motion to knock

142

my opponent off balance while keeping my feet firmly planted. Ironically, Texas native George Foreman began his illustrious boxing career in 1969 and I practiced some of his moves. My quickness in setting up, coupled with a Foreman boxer-type move, was my only hope for survival against Deacon.

A reporter from the *Dallas Morning News* named Frank Luksa approached me that week and asked, "Rayfield, how do you plan on blocking Deacon Jones this week? He's mobile, agile and hostile!" I replied, "You know what, Frank? I'm mobile, agile and hostile, too!"

Game day finally arrived. Upon entering LA Coliseum, I was composed on the outside but nervous as hell on the inside. I wasn't so much afraid, just anxious to do my best for the team. Most people facing challenges probably experience the same emotion. It's all about doing your best. Coach Myers approached me in the locker room and asked, "Are you ready to play, Rayfield?" *Play? This wasn't going to be a game of checkers, man!* "Coach," I stated, "if the game isn't going to be cancelled, then I'm ready to go to work."

We won the coin toss and elected to receive. Staubach called our first play from the huddle and I headed towards the line of scrimmage for my first face-to-face with Deacon. Getting into my well-rehearsed stance, I slowly lifted my head to find eyes of fire penetrating through me. They were hungry eyes, and Deacon looked as though I was going to be his first meal of the month. With just mere inches separating us, I could feel his hot breath on my face. He kicked back his foot like a bull ready to charge. But he wasn't a bull. He was a *massive ram*—ready to knock my ass through the goal post. It only took seconds, perhaps a fraction of a second, but the play unfolded in slow motion.

Immediately before the ball was snapped on the second "hut," I heard a deep, booming voice say, "Boy, do your mamma know you're out here?" The words were

so grave and powerful they snapped my concentration. Failing to hear Staubach call the second hut or an audible, I remained mesmerized in my stance, the play long forgotten. Deacon raged across the scrimmage line and flattened me with the force of a beer truck. I lay on my back, pained and totally embarrassed, yet thankful that the play was away from my side of

The destructive Deacon Jones.
Photo by Pro Look.

the field. Rolling onto my side and looking dazed towards the sideline, I watched as Coach Landry casually turned away from my pleading eyes. *Ouch! That look hurt me more than Deacon's hit.*

Coming out of my trance, I looked up to see Deacon's powerful, head-slappin' arm extending down towards me. Jokingly he said, "Hey, rookie, welcome to the NFL!" Looking up into those crimson eyes, I slapped his hand away and exclaimed, "First of all, Mr. Jones, you don't know my mother, so don't ever talk about her! And if this is how you want to play the game today, then bring it on and let's play!" Refusing his assistance, I got up and headed towards the huddle thinking, *Man! This guy can hit! It's going to be a helluva long day.*

We lost the game by one point but Deacon Jones never touched our quarterback that afternoon. Walking off the field, he approached me and said, "Hey, man! Great game! And I really wasn't talkin' about your mother."

"Thank you, sir," was my exhausted response.

★

The game against Deacon that day was a substantial turning point in my career. I was presented with the game ball and honored as the Oak Farms Most Valuable Player. Finishing the season as a starter, I earned honorable mention for the All-Pro team. Shortly thereafter, Gil Brandt called wanting to renegotiate my contract. Coach Lomax's presence was certainly missed, but his spirit was with me. My base salary was increased to $25,000 with a more lucrative incentive package. After successfully ending our season with an 11-2-1 record, I couldn't wait for the next season to begin.

The Beginning of a Dynasty
1970

Monday Night Football began in the fall of 1970. At the same time, a new chapter was being charted for the Cowboys history books. Their first draft choice was a jewel named Duane Thomas, a running back from West Texas State. Steve Kiner, a linebacker from Tennessee, was selected in the third round. Most players thought Duane and Steve were a little different. Since they were of a new generation and not afraid to test the system, they were considered rebels and free spirits. The veterans were settled in their ways and acquainted with the system so they never tried to challenge it. Surprisingly enough, players in this new generation had no fear of losing their job, being traded or being blackballed.

Duane Thomas was a smooth player on the field.

Seeing an attitude change within the organization, I recall Duane and Steve becoming the first integrated roommates whenever the team traveled. This was great to see because during my first three years there were always 13 black players on the team. Whenever we traveled, I was always in a room by myself. I assumed it was because my last name started with a"W."Yet there were 40 players total, meaning that one white player also had a separate room. I sometimes wondered why I wasn't placed with *that* team member, but then I didn't spend a lot of time trying to figure it out.

Other players joining the team were Bob Asher, an offensive tackle from Vanderbilt; a fast wide receiver from Henderson Junior College named Margene Adkins; Charlie Waters, a defensive back from Clemson; John Fitzgerald, an offensive tackle from Boston College; defensive end Pat Toomay from Vanderbilt; Joe Williams, a running back from Wyoming; and defensive back Mark Washington from Morgan State.

★

Coach Landry and John Niland share a moment.

I was selected as the starting right tackle. Ralph Neely's ankle had healed so they moved him to right guard. With John Niland and Tony Liscio covering the left side and Dave Manders at center, the offensive line appeared to be rock solid. After a few games, it became clear that Ralph wanted to play tackle and, since Liscio was ready for retirement, the coaches moved Ralph to left tackle and Blaine Nye, a defensive tackle from Stanford, stepped into the offensive guard position. This transition would produced an unrelenting line.

★

That November, during a Monday night game with Don Meredith in the broadcast booth, we found our record slip to 5-4 after being annihilated by the St. Louis

Cardinals 38-0. The media began to speculate that our chances at another playoff looked uninviting, but we won our last five games to claim the Eastern Division, which put us in the playoffs for the fifth consecutive season. In one memorable playoff, we hosted the Detroit Lions and their legendary tackle Alex Karras. Our Doomsday Defense kept them locked up all day. Can you believe that, after 60 minutes of professional football, only a safety and a field goal were scored? Our 5-0 victory remains one of the lowest scores in NFL history.

This was the first season after the AFL merged with the NFL. The realignment put the Cowboys in the NFC Eastern Division with the Giants, Cardinals, Eagles and Redskins. The NFC Championship game was against the 49ers. The flight to San Francisco was uneventful until we approached the city. The plane was preparing to touch down when all of the sudden the nose of the plane shot straight up. I mean *fast and hard*. It seems as though we had an extremely close call with another aircraft on the runway. The game would prove to be even more turbulent.

Candlestick Park was packed with almost 60,000 spectators. I still remember hearing Johnny Mathis perform the national anthem. Late in the fourth quarter, we had the ball with mere seconds remaining on the clock. Leading 17-10, we continued getting first downs to control the ball while the clock ran out. Suddenly, a fight started and unruly fans began inundating the field. Then brawls broke out everywhere—it was total chaos. Cautiously heading towards the locker room, I noticed

I was serious about the game.

Gil Brandt being bullied by some fans so I helped him

through the commotion. (Before joining the Cowboys, Gil was a baby portrait photographer. So I figured he lacked fighting skills and could use an escort off the field.) Players can usually duke it out among themselves, but when fans get involved it can lead to serious consequences.

Coach Landry instilled in us the belief that the *offense will win the game and the defense will win championships.* We validated his convictions that year. Our defense was on a roll, making it difficult for our opponents to score while our offense continued putting just enough points on the board.

Super Bowl V

The victory over the 49ers gave the Cowboys their first NFC title and a trip to Super Bowl V in Miami for a chance to win the coveted Lombardi Trophy. Our opponents were the Baltimore Colts, whose coaching leadership changed the year before from Don Shula to Don *Easy Rider* McCafferty. Quarterback Johnny Unitas was their fearless leader. Two years earlier, the Colts lost to the Jets in Super Bowl III, giving the National League its first loss in the title game.

The game was two weeks away and there was a pulsating excitement within the organization. Our team

Player-turned-coach Dan Reeves. Photo by Bob Lilly.

stayed in Dallas that first week as we continued our practices and preparations. My time was spent studying a great defensive end named Big Bubba Smith, an All-Pro who had certainly made his mark in the NFL (and on several of his opponents). Standing 6-foot-9 and weighing close to 300 pounds, his power rush appeared to be twice as strong as any other end in the league and his legendary headslap left many players senseless. After studying films of him, I kept telling myself that *I couldn't let him get control or establish power moves against me.* Coach Myers told me the key was to get to his chest quickly and use all of my strength to control him, otherwise, he could destroy our quarterback. I spent extra time after practice to prepare for what was to be my most mentally and physically challenging game yet.

Arriving in Miami a week before the game, the atmosphere was charged and our team's excitement escalated to even greater heights. There were festivities, parties and interviews by media outlets from around the world. Bob Hayes was back in his home state. Dan Reeves, who had joined our coaching staff, was from the neighboring state of Georgia. We had team meetings each morning and rigorous practice sessions in the afternoons. Coach Landry, in true disciplinarian fashion, enforced an 11 p.m. curfew all week.

Scrimmage At Sea

After a quick meeting and light workout Saturday morning, we were given free time for the rest of the day. Mel Renfro, Larry Cole, Phil Clark, Dick Daniels, Ron East and I went deep-sea fishing. We chartered a boat, hired a fishing guide, loaded a cooler with beer and headed 10-15 miles out to sea for what should have been a relaxing afternoon in the Florida sunshine.

For some reason the captain could sense that, when it came to deep-sea fishing, we were all rookies. Once we arrived at our destination, he had us bait our hooks and cast them into the water. With two chairs on the top deck and four on the lower deck, I settled in the left corner seat on the bottom deck. We were chillin', drinking beer and having a great time when a report came over the radio about a huge catch made about five miles from our boat. While we were joking about killer whales and great white sharks, the captain pointed toward my side of the boat and shouted, "Whoa! There comes one!" Peering into the crystal clear water, we saw the flash of a dark, long sea creature. The captain shouted to "Get back to your chairs, pick up your rod and reels and brace yourselves!" We dropped our beer cans like a bad fumble and followed his command. I watched the fish reappear and make a swift turn. Suddenly, my line began taking off. *zzzzeeee!* I hollered for the captain, who immediately helped secure my line and I braced myself accordingly. "Let the fish run with the line for a while. He'll eventually tire out." The captain reminded me not to let go of the reel. Well, that much I knew.

I patiently sat there for over an hour before the captain told me to start reeling the line in a little at a time and "Don't fight the fish." Each time I tightened the line, the fish would take off. *zzzzeeee!* He sure was messin' with me. My arms were getting tired. I asked one of the guys to help me, but the captain advised against it. He said I had to "Let the fish go or bring him in yourself." *Obviously, the captain didn't understand the team-sport concept.* My teammates looked on as they continued drinking beer and soaking up the rays.

Another two and a half hours passed before the fish was near enough to the boat for us to see. It was magnificent! The captain pulled out a gaff, reached down into the water and hooked the fish in its side before pulling it up into the boat. It was a sailfish, part of the marlin family, measuring seven feet long and weighing

From left, Phil Clark, Ron East, Larry Cole, Rayfield Wright, Mel Renfro and Dick Daniels.
We all agreed that catching footballs was easier than catching fish.

90 pounds. It was amazing to see something this big come out of the water. Its colors were beautiful—that of a rainbow! The remarkable part of this catch was the fish never swallowed the bait! I had hooked it around its gill. Once the fish was stowed, I realized that my arms were cramped and unmovable. Tackling this fish left me totally exhausted, so my teammates began massaging my arms in an effort to relieve the spasms. There was no way I was going to be able to play in the Super Bowl with my arms in this condition. I thought *this 90 pound fish kicked my butt after four hours*… what was Bubba Smith going to do to me without my arms being 100 percent?

The captain raised a flag to indicate our big catch on board and we headed back to shore. Arriving at the dock, we noticed a large crowd had gathered near another boat. We went to see what caused the commotion and discovered it to be an enormous 20-foot white hammerhead shark, hanging by its tail from the back of a wrecker. Its size, its teeth, everything about it, was awesome! Shaped like a hammer and weighing more than 1,000 pounds, there was nothing pretty about it.

Now that my fish seemed to be the size of a minnow, I had to decide whether to keep it or sell it (at the unbelievable price of $1,000!). Discovering that I could have it mounted and shipped to Dallas for $600, that was my choice. My teammates and I agreed that this was an experience of a lifetime. Back at the hotel, trainer Don Cochran examined my arms and thought my muscle spasms would be better the next day if I kept heat on them all night. Which is what I did.

Bowled Over

After breakfast and a short team meeting the next morning, we had a few hours to relax in our rooms before going to the stadium. My concentration was on one thing — big Bubba Smith. At the time, I never knew Bubba's first name but it had to be *Big*. When we finally came face-to-face, I thought to myself *My God! This guy's a monster! What am I in for today?* Needless to say, I had my hands full.

Even though Bob Hayes and Calvin Hill were injured, and the media was down on our performance, we were still favored to win the game by one point. Our only advantage was our ability to play on artificial turf. The teams battled throughout the day and suffered through 11 ugly turnovers, injuries and ill timing.

Two controversial plays could have affected the outcome of the game. The first was a pass from Johnny Unitas to intended receiver Eddie Hinton. As Hinton leaped for the ball, our defensive back Mel Renfro was also in the air. Hinton tipped the pass. Colts tight end and rambling man, John Mackey, caught the ball and ran in for the leading touchdown. League rules prohibit two receivers on the same team from touching the ball without a defender touching it in between. Yes, it *appeared* that Mel touched the ball. After watching the game films, I believe the play remains questionable. Without instant replay, the play stood as called.

The other conflict-ridden play came late in the fourth quarter. Tied at 13-13, we had the ball inside the 5-yard line preparing to score or, at the very least, kick a field goal to win the game. Coach Landry called a conservative play to run up the middle so we would at least be in field-goal position. Staubach handed off to Duane Thomas who had a great day running the ball. As always, in a short yardage and goal-line play, the middle stacks up quickly. Duane hit the line of scrimmage and the ball came loose. Our center, Dave Manders, ended up with the ball, but Colts tackle Billy Ray Smith jumped up from the pile and screamed "Colts ball!" while pointing in the opposite direction.

Center Dave Manders.
Photo by Bob Lilly.

The Colts were given possession, made a few great plays and, with seconds remaining on the clock, rookie kicker Jim O'Brien gave the Colts the Super Bowl title, 16-13.

After the game and out of sheer frustration, Bob Lilly threw his helmet 50 yards upfield. I know that wasn't Bob's style. He was frustrated. After 15 years of playing with the Cowboys, he just wanted a title.

Even though we lost, I was glad to see our Chuck Howley win the MVP award for making two interceptions and forcing a fumble. It was a rare occasion—granting the MVP to a player on the losing team—but it was well

 deserved. I think our players each received $7,500 for the appearance but it didn't seem worth it. It wasn't about money… it was about winning. And we still couldn't *win the big one*. Calling it the *Blunder Bowl*, the media reviews were relentless.

MVP Chuck Howley #54.

Our Sweet Six Team
1971

There was no question about it. Losing Super Bowl V was devastating for my teammates, the entire organization and me. Knowing we should have won that game left us with an empty feeling that carried over into our off-season training.

The Cowboys continued assembling multitalented athletes from around the country. The '71 draft brought four new players to the team. The No. 1 choice was a defensive end from Southern Cal, Tody Smith, Big Bubba Smith's *little* brother. Tody was only 6–5 and weighed 250 pounds. Other recruits included Isaac Thomas, a defensive back from Bishop College in Dallas; defensive end Bill Gregory from Wisconsin and Rodney Wallace, a defensive tackle from New Mexico who was later converted into an offensive tackle. Lance Rentzel, who had a record-setting 13 catches in one game, retired and was replaced by future Hall of Famer

Lance Rentzel.
Photo by Bob Lilly.

Lance *Bambi* Alworth.

Another example of the Cowboys *outside the box* scouting style was the signing of kicker Toni Fritsch. The scouts discovered Toni while he was playing soccer in Vienna, Austria. Through an interpreter, Toni watched his first video of a football game and immediately signed a contract he couldn't even read. I recall his showing up at camp with an interpreter. What a culture shock that must have been. I think Toni's first two words spoken in English were "Three points."

The last game played in the Cotton Bowl was a 20-13 win against the Giants. On October 24, 1971, we played our sixth game of the season against the New England Patriots (known at the time as the Boston Patriots). Being our first game in the state-of-the-art Texas Stadium, we were determined to send a message around the league that "If you're coming to our house to play, you better pack a lunch because it'll be a long day." Less than three minutes into the game, through an opening created by Blaine Nye and myself, Duane Thomas throttled his way

Coach Landry talking strategy with Craig Morton and Roger Staubach.

to a 56-yard touchdown to put the first six points on the board. The sellout crowd went wild!

Realizing he had two talented quarterbacks, Coach Landry began to alternate Craig Morton and Roger Staubach— first between games and then between plays. *Can you imagine this being done in today's NFL?* Because both players had their own style, this routine certainly made my job interesting. I always knew where Craig was going to be, whereas Roger loved to run and scramble. Keeping my finger on his pulse was sometimes a challenge. Finally, on November 7, Coach Landry assigned the starting position to Roger.

We dominated our last seven opponents to finish the season with an 11-3 record and won the Eastern Division title for the sixth consecutive year. Facing the Minnesota Vikings on the road, my great challenge was to block Carl Eller and Alan Page. We beat a tough Vikings team, led by quarterback Fran Tarkenton and head coach Bud Grant, 20-12.

Throughout the season, still tormented by the bitter effects of our Super Bowl V loss, we desperately wanted to win the world championship. More than anything, we wanted to shake the tag of not being able to win the big game. Facing San Francisco, we had the attitude and mind-set to accomplish that goal. As luck would have it, we defeated the 49ers (14-3) and became the NFC Champions for the second straight year. The Miami Dolphins earned the AFC privilege to travel to New Orleans for the ultimate title. The stage was set for Super Bowl VI. Dolphins Coach Don Shula and

Congratulating Cedrick Hardman on a hard-fought game.

our Coach Landry were longtime friends. Coach Landry had us focused and poised to bring home the title... in spite of the distractions surrounding us.

The most important component of our game preparation was to focus on nullifying Miami's defense. Our offensive plan included some difficult and deceptive running plays. Late in the first quarter, both teams were playing competitively. Then our Doomsday Defense got their game on and began shutting down the Dolphins'

159

offense. This gave our offense the confidence to score some points and gain control of the football. With our defense playing extremely well, our offense dominated the second half with Staubach doing what he did best. The running talents of Duane Thomas and Walt Garrison contributed to the game. They performed brilliantly as the offensive line executed with style.

As the sun went down over Tulane Stadium that evening, the Dallas Cowboys also went down—in history—with a winning score of 24-3. We had captured our first Super Bowl title and set a Super Bowl record for the most rushing yards (252).

★

I had never in my life rejoiced in such sweet victory. Roger Staubach was named MVP and I earned my first All-

Coach Landry had a lot to smile about as Mel Renfro (#20) and I (#70) carried him off the field.

Pro honor. Having played offensive tackle for just two years, I was elated. Arriving in Dallas the next morning, the fans paid us tribute with an elaborate parade. We also had the opportunity to thank them for their continued support. Oh, and the media was there in force, with some very nice things to say for a change!

As we gathered around City Hall, the Dallas mayor presented each team member with a signed and sealed proclamation that stated: *"In view of these and their many, many other achievements in the world of professional sports, the Dallas Cowboys have won for themselves enduring affection from the citizens of Dallas. They are hereby welcome home from the world's championship professional football game with accolades for their dedication to excellence in athletic competition."* That experience will always be etched in my mind.

★

Winning the world title presented some of the players, especially black players, with promising career and business opportunities. Coach Myers introduced me to John Gray, President of National Bank of Commerce in downtown Dallas. The interview went well and I was offered a job. I entered the officer's training program and began learning the vital elements of each department. My goal was to learn every aspect of finance, banking and investments. This was a very significant step in my life.

Also that summer, Jethro Pugh, Pat Toomay and I were appointed to a goodwill tour throughout the Far East with the Air Force. In a way, it was reminiscent of a Bob Hope tour. Our first stop was at Hickam Air Force base on the Hawaiian island of Oahu. From there we went to Guam, Okinawa, Yukota, Tokyo, Osan and Kuson. Our tour concluded with stops in Seoul, South Korea, and the Philippine Islands.

For the first time I caught a glimpse of what my life would have been like had I gone into the service. The men and women who serve our country are the real heroes. They should have been on tour—not me. After all, I was just a football player. Supporting U.S. troops was personally satisfying for me. Being my first time abroad, experiencing cultures whose religious beliefs, foods and governments were so different from those in America, were priceless.

Defending The Title
1972

The introduction of the Dallas Cowboys Cheerleaders further increased the popularity of the NFL and amplified the marketing of our team and the league. As the reigning world champs, we began '72 filled with optimism. But early on we lost Lilly and Staubach to injuries. Our defense, led by powerhouse Lee Roy Jordan, was solid, and my job on offense was to help keep our opponents out of Craig Morton's pockets. Tight end Mike Ditka, who joined us in 1969 from Chicago, was making a transition from player to special-teams coach. Rookie Jean Fugett, an energetic tight end from Amherst, and Billy Truax, acquired

The dynamic Jean Fugett.

from the Rams in a trade, competed for the open position. Naturally, I would have treasured the opportunity to become a tight end, but the coaches felt my abilities at offensive tackle were just beginning to materialize. And little did I know that my star was ready to shine over one of the finest seasons of my career.

Gil Brandt continued finding gifted players such as running backs Robert Newhouse from Houston and Bill Thomas from Boston College; linebackers John Babinecz out of Villanova, Houston's Mike Keller and Ralph Coleman from North Carolina and Utah punter Marv Bateman. The team also signed Ron Sellers and traded the divisive Duane Thomas to San Diego for Billy Parks and Mike Montgomery.

In our first game, Morton's passes successfully soared to Ron Sellers and Lance Alworth as we clipped the Eagles, 28-6. The next week our Doomsday Defense belittled the Giants as we put another tally in the win

column. Ends Larry Cole and Pat Toomay had big performances that day. Week 3 found Green Bay packin' enough serious heat to beat us, 16-13. Linebackers Chuck Howley and D. D. Lewis helped us take away a victory from our next opponents, the Pittsburgh Steelers. I recall Cornell Green intercepting a Terry Bradshaw pass, and Calvin Hill twisting the Steelers' defense

Cornell Green could have starred in the NBA.
Photo by Bob Lilly.

out of kilter when he threw an unpredictable touchdown from his tailback position. The next Sunday in Baltimore, tackle Jethro Pugh helped stifle the Colts' offense as Craig Morton put on a show in a 21-0 shutout.

When I think of the bitter rivalry between the Cowboys and the Washington Redskins, I try to figure out why we had such an abiding dislike for one another. I think it was because we were both competitive. The challenges from both sides of the bench were extremely emotional, powerful, physical. One of Coach Landry's greatest sayings was, "When you want to win a game, you have to teach. When you lose a game, you have to learn." Each game made us better—as a team and as individuals. Just like people are blessed with individual personalities, so are NFL teams. Speaking for myself, I've always respected the Redskins. Even Coach George Allen with his *The Future Is Now* motto.

During this particular game, we took two 13-point leads but Washington rallied to a 24-20 triumph. I guess we learned a lot that day!

Continuing the season, we won some games and lost others. We eventually developed a distressing undercurrent among our statistics: in a four-game span, we allowed nearly 100 points mainly in the second half. We were getting a reputation of being *30-minute champions*. In spite of all that, we qualified for the playoffs (for the seventh consecutive season) as the wild-card team with a 10-4 record.

★

Since wild-card teams traveled, we flew to San Francisco to face the the 49ers at Candlestick Park. We had defeated them the past two years for the NFC crown, so we expected a vicious grudge match. They threw the first punch as Vic Washington returned the opening kickoff 97 yards for a touchdown. They remained the heavyweight until the last two minutes of the game. Down 28-16, Staubach connected with Billy Parks for a 20-yard TD that cut the deficit to 28-23. With 80 seconds remaining, an onside kickoff was our only hope. Toni Fritsch's behind-the-back boot bounced off Preston Riley and landed in the gifted hands of Mel Renfro. From the 50-yard line, Coach Landry sent in the next play and, believe me, he didn't call for Staubach to scrap and scramble for 21 yards! But that's exactly what Roger did. From the 29-yard line, with 63

Mel Renfro was a sprinter when he was discovered.
Photo by Bob Lilly.

seconds left, Billy Parks pulled in another pass taking us to the 10. After this sequence of miracles, with 56 seconds on the clock, Roger reached back for one more. His pass to Ron Sellers for the winning touchdown was perfect to climax a 30-28 victory.

I've played more than 200 professional football games and that one remains high on my top 10 list among the most memorable. Even the 26-3 loss to the Redskins one week later for the NFC Championship didn't dampen our accomplishments. (OK… maybe it did… just a little.)

★

Although the season ended for the Cowboys, I faced one more game. For the second year, I was elected to the NFC All-Pro team and headed to Miami for my first Pro Bowl appearance. Upon hearing the news, I felt as

I was having one of the best seasons of my career.

though I had reached the highest peak possible. The Pro Bowl players surrounding me was humbling. *Immensely talented players!* From the AFC there was Joe Namath, Larry Csonka, Franco Harris, Otis Taylor, O.J. Simpson, Art Shell, Deacon Jones, Mean Joe Greene and Gene Upshaw. The NFC sported Walt Garrison, Calvin Hill, Charley Taylor, Bob Lilly, Merlin Olsen, Alan Page, Dick Butkus, Coy Bacon (who was now with the Rams), Mel Renfro and Cornell Green. Those were the days of truly great players.

I always thought that receiving All-Pro honors would be the pinnacle of a football career. But the mountain proved to be higher than I first imagined when I was named the 1972 NFC Offensive Lineman Of The Year. Knowing that my peers, such as the ones listed above and NFL coaches voted for me to receive this honor put me on top of the world. Praise God!

I flew to New York City for the awards ceremony, where I met Larry Little, the AFC Offensive Lineman Of The Year. A guard for the Miami Dolphins, Larry went to Bethune–Cookman College. Similar to Fort Valley, Bethune was a low-profile college in the SIAC Conference. Larry and I were small-town kids who grew up without the luxuries of $100 tennis shoes, designer clothes and summer football camps. We had something much more priceless—a deeply instilled desire to give the game our best.

★

Many players didn't pursue summer employment; they just relaxed and enjoyed themselves until it was time for summer training camp. I always thought that would have been nice to release all my cares and responsibilities for a few months. But at the age of 6, I learned the meaning and importance of hard work so I continued working during the off-season. It wasn't about the money. It was about life. More importantly, it was about life after football.

Even though I had my degree in education, I continued seeking knowledge in many areas of business. I studied mortgage banking, investments, real estate, marketing and communications. NFL players have relatively short careers. I had no idea that I was going to play for 13 years! Back in the seventies, a player's career lasted less than four years on average. Today, it's *less than three years*. Therefore, it's important for players to make the best of the game while they're playing. With the amount of money players are making today, financial management is imperative, and players should be smart about their decisions. One thing I wanted to accomplish during this time was to secure my family and myself financially and determine

my career path for life after football.

★

Something extraordinary happened in 1972 that made NFL history. The Miami Dolphins, who we defeated in the Super Bowl the previous season, prevailed with *a perfect season*. No other franchise has accomplished such an amazing achievement. I salute the Dolphins coaches and players who made this historic event possible—especially their No-Name Defense. In particular, my friend Larry Little. Other Dolphins superstars were Coach Shula, Larry Csonka, Bob Griese, Nick Buoniconti, Marv Fleming, Manny Fernandez, Bob Kuechenberg, Earl Morrall, Jim Kiick, Jake Scott, Mercury Morris and Paul Warfield. I'd be remiss if I failed to mention Vern Den Herder and Bill Stanfill, Miami's great defensive ends! Congratulations, gentlemen. I am honored to have played the game with all of you.

Promising Players & Answered Prayers
1973

September 24 was a celebrated day in Cowboys history. Our 40-3 triumph over New Orleans gave Coach Landry his 100th victory, placing him at No. 8 among NFL coaches with the most wins. The honor was well earned and I was proud of Coach Landry and his entire coaching staff.

With 10 rookies incorporated into our system, their enthusiasm blended nicely with the wisdom of our veterans. I noticed exceptional talent in Billy Joe DuPree from Michigan State and Dallas native Harvey Martin. There was Bruce

Billy Joe DuPree was a great addition to our team.

Walton, closely resembling his brother, Bill, of basketball fame. Rodrigo Barnes from Rice was another standout. With due respect to other linebackers, I personally thought Rodrigo was the best linebacker for us. Something great happened every time he was on the field so it was unfortunate that he stayed just two years. The Cowboys doors sometimes revolved like a .38 special.

Bob Hayes, who had a knack for nicknames, dubbed me *Big Cat*. I hope my feline agility and quickness helped us average a phenomenal 30 points a game in our first seven match-ups. Our offense was masterful with the talents of Bob Hayes, Mike Montgomery, Golden Richards

and free agent Drew Pearson, a high school teammate of Joe Theismann. I remember the power of Walt Garrison and the determination of Calvin Hill

Calvin Hill #35 played with determination.

who, for the second consecutive year, gained more than 1,000 yards, scrapping and squirming for every inch. Nor was there a substitute for my fullback buddy Robert Newhouse."House"was a solid player who never missed a beat.

By mid-season, we had mustered a 4-3 record. I wasn't too ashamed of our standing because it was the same as we had in 1971, the year we won Super Bowl VI. Then we won our next three games. On a mission, we met the Dolphins who were defending their Super Bowl title and perfect season from '72. Our hopes were chapped early in the game as we kissed away a 14-7 loss. Facing Denver the next

Clearing a path for Robert Newhouse.

Sunday, we were on a quest with a new deceptive play up our sleeves. It was an unusual rollout that singled out a setback and a tight end. Naturally, the Broncos covered the setback and Staubach connected with the tight end. I figured it was foolproof… and it was. We tried it again the following week, with even greater success, against the puzzled Redskins in a 27-7 rout.

In the end, we rode our way back to the playoffs for

an NFL record-breaking eighth consecutive year. Before a sellout crowd in Dallas, we showed the NFC champ LA Rams everything but mercy during a 27-16 victory. The following week the Minnesota Vikings came to our house to battle for a trip to the Super Bowl. What a tough clash. Losing 27-10 on our own turf was devastating.

★

Although I had a *meanness* on the gridiron, I've always had a gentle compassion towards children. For many years, I have made time to support youth organizations so it wasn't unusual that summer to accept an invitation to film a commercial for Foster Parents. I arrived at the studio, had my hair and makeup done and went through the script. It was a piece of cake. The director got me situated in front of the cameras, adjusted the lighting and we were ready to roll. Before the first take, a woman approached me and gently cradled two babies in my arms. As I studied their beautiful faces, my eyes focused immediately on their eyes. Have you ever looked deep into the eyes of a baby? They capture your soul and speak to your heart with a divine innocence. It didn't take long to realize that man didn't put that divineness there... and man cannot take it away. Not only did I see their eyes, I saw their souls and felt their spirits. I thought "Oh my God!" as the most amazing sensation spiraled through my heart faster than a Staubach pass.

I was so touched holding these blessed gifts that it took me several takes to eventually get through filming the commercial. I was moved as these babies remained focused on me with all the love and innocence in the world. Finally, when I was able to finish, it was not easy to give the babies back. As I hesitantly handed them to the counselor, I asked, "Do these beautiful children need parents and a home?"

She replied, "Yes."

"I would like to be their father."

"To which one?" she asked.

"Both children," was my answer.

When I went home that evening, I told my wife Andrea about the babies and explained how they, through the spirit of God, had captured my heart. Since we didn't have children of our own, we knew it would be a blessing from God to unite them with our lives. Our first sacred gift was the little boy who we named LaRay, 'La' from Larry and 'Ray' from Rayfield. Our next Godsend was the little girl named Anitra... taken from Andrea's name.

LaRay recently graduated from SMU with a Master's degree in Business Administration. Anitra majored in Biochemical Engineering at Harvard. Being their father is a blessing and an honor.

My children have been a life's blessing.

★

Cowboys Under Construction
1974

Each year a transfusion of players was introduced to our team. As a veteran, I could feel the new blood circulating through our veins while the experience and talent of the veterans kept the heart of our team strong. Some positions remained weak, but the Cowboys made a bold move to strengthen our defense when they traded Tody Smith and Billy Parks to the Houston Oilers for the right to pick first in the draft. They subsequently used that pick to select Ed 'Too Tall' Jones, a defensive end from Tennessee State. Along with Too Tall, our lifeline was revived when the team acquired Charlie Young, running back from North Carolina; Danny White, quarterback from Arizona State; Western Illinois defensive back Dennis Morgan; tackle Gene Killian from Tennessee; and linebackers Ken Hutcherson from Livingston State and Calvin Peterson from UCLA. Calvin played a few years, then returned to California to appear in the movie *Heaven Can Wait* with Jim Boeke, Deacon Jones and Jack Snow, as players, and film-star Warren Beatty.

Our opening game against Atlanta was superbly played and the 24-0 shutout was a confidence-builder. But our blocks tumbled as we lost the next four games. With a 1-4 record, we were in last place in the NFC East. We finished 8-6 and, for the first time in eight years, the Cowboys were denied a trip to the playoffs. (This would be the only year in the decade of the '70s where we failed to qualify.) In spite of our trials, there were many shining stars on our team. I vividly remember

Giving Robert Newhouse #44 room to run.

Dennis Morgan. During one of his first games as a rookie, he ran a 98-yard punt return against the Cardinals. Big plays like that gave us hope that we could return to the playoffs. Our offense was proud of the fact that we had tallied more yards than any team in the NFL. Once again, I was voted Offensive Lineman of the Year in the NFC and was headed for my third consecutive Pro Bowl game.

There were two remarkable games that year against the Redskins that die-hard football fans still ask me about. During the first challenge, we were down by four touchdowns at the half. Doomsday Defense came out slugging in the second half with Green, Renfro, Toomay, Cole and Pugh. Lilly, Jordan, Lewis and Edwards also put up a great fight. Too Tall and Harvey Martin paired up their talents. As we tried to disconnect the Redskins' energy,

Roger Staubach takes a major hit.

the forces of Robert Newhouse and Billy Joe DuPree cut the lead to seven points. At fourth and goal, trailing 28-21 in the last few seconds, Staubach found Drew Pearson at the post but the pass deflected off his shoulder pad. My heart ached for Pearson.

On Thanksgiving Day, we sought retribution at Texas Stadium. Down 16-3 going into the second half, our chances of avenging our earlier loss took a hit when the Redskins left Roger dazed, confused and sidelined with a concussion. Rookie Clint Longley came to the huddle as quarterback without any type of pro experience or even a warm up pass. Odds were against us but his wits and strong arm united with Billy Joe DuPree for a rapid seven points. With 35 seconds left in the game, we were down 23-17 with the ball on the 50-yard line. I saw confidence in the faces of the Redskins defenders, but it faded when Longley connected with Pearson for the 24-23 victory. Longley would become an instant hero.

Ah! Football doesn't get much better than that.

★

Bob Lilly, known around the country as Mr. Cowboy, was a stallion of a player who retired at the end of this season. He was the first Cowboy drafted into the organization, and the only player remaining on the team since the inception of the franchise in 1960. A catalyst on the defensive line, Bob's star shined for 14 years and he started every game of his career—a Cowboy record still

Bob Lilly captivated fans and captured pictures.
Photo by George Andrie.

unmatched today. I know he must have suffered the usual aches and pains but he never complained. In fact, he taped his own knees before each game, declining offers from the trainers. That was amazing to me. What a mountain of a man!

It was also intriguing that this tough guy chose photography as one of his hobbies. He captured many candid, and some not-so-candid, pictures of the team's

early years… many of which you are viewing within the second half of this book. Being co-captains together, we became good friends and I'm still blessed to have him in my life today.

Bob and I have remained good friends for more than 35 years.
Photo by Ann Lilly.

Departures and the Dirty Dozen
1975

Several players who helped lead us to the playoffs in eight of the previous nine years were gone. With the departure of Lilly, Garrison, Reeves, Hayes, Niland, Manders and Calvin Hill, critics thought our journey toward our 10th playoff berth would be shaky. But the organization remained clever in its scouting. Building for the future, Dallas recruited more rookies than ever. After being cut by the Steelers, halfback Preston Pearson found a home with the Cowboys. By

Randy "The Manster" White.

trading Craig Morton to the Giants, we received two first-round draft choices. Our first selection was Randy White, a brute and bruiser from Maryland. The second first-round pick was linebacker Thomas Henderson from Langston College.

The Cowboys drafted gifted Burton Lawless, an offensive guard from Florida; linebackers Bob Bruenig from Arizona State and Mike Hegman from Too Tall's

177

alma matter of Tennessee State; Pat Donovan, a Stanford grad who played defensive end; and Oklahoma's Randy Hughes and Kyle Davis. Mitch Hoopes signed on, as did Herb Scott, Scott Laidlaw and Rolly Woolsey. Since there were 12 rookies, they were dubbed the *Dirty Dozen*. In due course, nine eventually became starters.

With a mixture of young and old, we had the experience and enthusiasm to saddle up and ride all the way to the Super Bowl. Our first rival was the Rams who butted across midfield just once. Doomsday had its game on. The next week we denied the Cardinals a victory when rookie 'Hollywood' Henderson flew 97 yards for a spectacular kickoff return touchdown. Our next victory, over the Lions, was a celebration with the defense sacking Detroit quarterbacks an amazing 11 times.

Oddly enough, it was our first year since the '66 season without a game on Thanksgiving Day. Our offense was improving and Staubach, although sometime unpredictable, was in his element. Being Cowboys, it was only fitting when Coach Landry reintroduced the *shotgun formation* to our team. This structure allowed Roger to have more time to read the defense and

Protecting Roger was my job.

made him less vulnerable to the pass rush. He loved it. And the shotgun brought even more challenge to my position of offensive tackle… which I thoroughly enjoyed.

★

As a team united, we fought our way to a 10-4 record, making us a wild-card team in the playoffs. We traveled to Minnesota for a visit with the "Purple People Eaters". The Vikings' vaunted defensive line of Jim Marshall, Carl Eller, Alan Page and Gary Larsen awaited. With 44 seconds on the game clock, their fans thought the 14-10 score was in the bag and began leaving the stadium. We were on our 25-yard line, fourth down and 16 to go. Staubach connected with Drew Pearson who stepped out of bounds on the 50-yard line. Two incomplete passes later, we found a mere 24 seconds remaining on the clock.

The next play was historic. Roger, back in the shotgun, heaved a long pass down the right sideline. It has been said *I drove Carl Eller all the way from Bloomington to Minneapolis* to give Staubach time to read the defense. That statement still brings a smile to my face. As I finished blocking Carl, I followed the trail of the ball and watched as intended receiver Drew Pearson crashed

Drew Pearson was full of grace on the playing field.

into Nate Wright at the 5-yard line. Nate fell to the ground as Drew miraculously locked the ball between his elbow and hip and made his way across the goal line. We won the game 17-14. It was another Cowboys comeback.

The crowd was angry because there wasn't a flag on the play. One spectator threw a whiskey bottle from the stands that hit an official in the head. Drew was getting trash and beer thrown at him. Fearing for his safety, Jethro and I escorted Drew, now known as Mr. Clutch, through the rowdy group of fans and into the locker room.

During the postgame press conference, and meaning no disrespect to his Catholic faith, Roger called the pass a *Hail Mary*. It was undeniably divine.

★

On January 4, we were underdogs when we faced the Rams in the NFC Championship Game. We knew that we could beat them (as we had earlier in the season) and wanted to prove it to the 80,000 fans that filled LA Coliseum. Successfully blocking Jack Youngblood was my greatest mission. Shutting down Fred Dryer was Neely's. Fitzgerald, Nye and Lawless remained tight in the middle. Preston Pearson's three touchdown receptions of 18, 15 and 19 yards were a huge contribution to the outcome. Our 37-7 conquest indicated a blowout, but it was a hard-hitting game. Rams Coach Chuck Knox was admired throughout the league and displayed respect toward his players. A true team coach, I would have enjoyed playing under his guidance.

Dreams of winning our second Super Bowl in six years were within our grasp. We were the first wild-

D. D. Lewis #50 locks in on Terry Bradshaw #12.

card team to arrive at a Super Bowl as we faced Chuck Noll's Pittsburgh Steelers. The Steelers were led by Terry Bradshaw, who generaled a team of John Stallworth, Lynn Swann, Franco Harris and others. Their Steel Curtain defense included Mean Joe Greene, L.C. Greenwood, Dwight White and Ernie Holmes up front; Jack Lambert, Jack Ham and Mel Blount appeared as hardened reinforcements. Tied 7-7 at the end of the first quarter, neither offense made tracks until our kicker, Toni Fritsch, booted a 36-yard field goal right before the half for a 10-7 lead.

In the locker room at halftime, we reviewed our strategies and re-established our focus on execution. We felt confident of winning the title and were optimistic that the next time we entered the room it would be as champions. It was a scoreless, hard-fought third quarter until the unexpected happened. I was in the huddle waiting for the next play from Coach Landry. (During these timeouts, offensive linemen would huddle and discuss the change-ups in the defense.) In the far distance, I was aware of an uproar coming from the crowd while I remained focused in our battle and on my trials with L.C. Greenwood and Mean Joe Greene.

Trying to catch my breath, hands upon my knees, looking at the turf, I suddenly noticed a pair of tiny feet standing directly in front of mine. Obviously, they didn't belong to a football player. Slowly following the feet upward, I was stunned to see a very well endowed, provocatively dressed young lady. As I began to stand, she promptly kissed my helmet and quickly placed something in my hand. It was some type of charm. I hastily flung it towards the sidelines just as rapidly as the security guards approached to escort her from the field.

My teammates looked at me with doubts and accusations but, honestly, I had no earthly idea who she was, where she came from, or why she was there. *Perhaps Deacon sent her!*

This charmer delivered some bad luck.

After all, he was the only other person on the gridiron to ever destroy my mental concentration.

Until this bizarre occurrence happened, the game was a head-to-head match-up. Beginning in the fourth quarter, things deteriorated for us as the Steel Curtain slowly pulled the cord on our dreams of winning. We were on our own goal line, couldn't make the first down and had to punt. It was blocked and trickled into the end zone for a safety. Punting to the Steelers, our defense kept them from a touchdown but they scored on a 36-yard kick by Roy Gerela for a 12-10 lead. The Steelers capped the game with a deep pass from Bradshaw to Lynn Swann for a 64-yard touchdown with minutes to spare. This score, along with a 161-yard game that earned Swann a well-deserved MVP award, gave the Steelers their second consecutive world title, 21-17.

★

The World Football League (WFL) was new to the football landscape and added exciting twists to the game. Teams named the Houston Texans, Jacksonville Sharks, Detroit Wheels, Philadelphia Bell and Hawaii Hawaiians played exciting games with a yellow and cobalt blue football. Goal posts were placed at the back of the end zone and TDs were worth seven points. There was no such thing as a fair catch. Twenty games were played each season on Wednesday and Saturday nights. Thursday was TV night. The WFL was alluring to some, while other critics found fault with the system.

The introduction of the WFL was gaining in popularity and had a reputation of handing out big bucks to NFL players. This added a spark to contract negotiations. Contract negotiations were always distracting for both players and coaches. Whether the contract was good or bad, attitudes and emotions were always involved. Agents representing players were becoming a new, popular concept and contracts were being reviewed much more closely.

I was in favor of the new league simply because it

I wanted to help children and those in need.

gave players an avenue to further their careers while, at the same time, it gave other talented, non-NFL athletes an opportunity to showcase their abilities. My thought was the WFL was healthy competition for the NFL and there was plenty of room for both.

Watching some veterans retire,

I began to contemplate the fact that I had played eight years, during which God had answered many of my prayers. At this point, I had been a starter for six years, voted NFC Offensive Lineman of the Year twice, made All Pro for the third time and played in my third Pro Bowl. Sports had been my world yet my heart believed I could still make a difference in the lives of others.

In the spring of 1975, Gil Brandt called me to his office to review my contract. Since 1967, I had always signed three-year contracts, which were always renegotiated before they expired. Prior to this meeting, I had the mindset of signing just one more agreement before hanging up my helmet.

During our meeting, Gil asked, "Rayfield, what would you like in your contract?" I replied, "Mr. Brandt, given my tenure and performance with the team and the organization, I want one million dollars for the next five years and a $75,000 signing bonus." Needless to say, he didn't take too kindly to my request. Taken aback, Gil exclaimed, "Why, we don't even pay Staubach that kind of money!" Granted, there wasn't any player on the team (that I was aware of) or in the NFL making that kind of money. However, a new sheriff was in the game and willing to pay the big bucks.

His answer, or rather the indirect answer he delivered from the higher-ups in the Cowboys organization, felt like a Bubba Smith forearm upside my head. That's all I needed to hear. Having no comment to Gil's nonchalant attitude, I left the room without saying a word.

★

In 1975, Abner Haynes, a former star of the Kansas City Chiefs and a close friend and confidant, and I were representing young athletes around the NFL and assisting with contract negotiations. We often talked about my contract and, even though I revealed certain elements of it to Abner, I still wanted to negotiate directly with the Cowboys. For nine years, my handshake with the Cowboys had been as solid as my word. That wasn't going to change.

Abner had contacts within the WFL. Within a matter of days after my meeting with Gil, Abner scheduled a meeting with William R. Putnam, owner of the WFL's Birmingham Americans. Jethro Pugh joined us on the trip to Atlanta but was unaware of the business meeting. Arriving at the Peachtree Marriott, Jethro went to his room to relax while Abner and I joined Mr. Putnam. First impressions are important to me, and Putnam appeared professional and successful. Cutting to the chase, I told him of my desires to support the WFL and to help build his team, which had just finished a 17-5 season. We agreed that, once I finished the remaining year on my Cowboys

Jethro Pugh.
Photo by Bob Lilly.

contract and an option year, I would join his club. The terms? Five years. One million dollars. And a $250,000 bonus the day I reported to Birmingham. He signed the future contract and handed me a check for $75,000. That alone was more than my yearly salary with the Cowboys. But the greatest incentive in the contract was priceless—the fact that I would also become an offensive coordinator for the team. *I would mentor and coach younger players to help them reach their full potential!* It was my ultimate dream.

I asked Mr. Putnam, "Would you be interested in offering a player like Jethro Pugh the same contract?"

"Sure!" he replied. "Let's call him on the phone and get him to Atlanta."

"He's already here at the hotel."

When the unsuspecting Jethro joined us, he was

shocked to learn I had just signed with the WFL. He became completely stunned when offered the exact same contract with the promise of becoming the teams defensive coordinator. Jethro promptly signed on the dotted line.

Some may wonder if I was selling out on my team by signing with the WFL. Absolutely not. I wanted to set a precedent in the sporting world with a message that there was room for other athletes to achieve their childhood dreams. Think about it. There were 26 teams in the NFL— 40 players per team—room enough for only 1,040 players in the league. There were thousands of gifted athletes deserving a chance to excel. With the addition of the WFL, I felt those athletes could also achieve greatness.

Other Cowboys signed with the WFL—Calvin Hill with the Hawaiians, Mike Montgomery with Birmingham, Danny White with Toronto. Nevertheless, the league was unable to establish a major television contract and folded in October of 1975.

In the end, the Cowboys offered me a five-year contract for $700,000—close to what I had originally asked.

★

Coaches & Captains
1976

NFL history was made with the introduction of the Tampa Bay Buccaneers and Seattle Seahawks into the league. Referees were now wearing microphones during the games and 30-second clocks became visible to both players and fans. Some prestigious coaches left their cleat prints on the league in 1976. Lou Holtz, for example, coached the New York Jet for 13 games. Like me, Coach Holtz grew up without material things and his parents separated early on. His dismal 3-10 season was a pivotal point in his career because losing changed his mental attitude. He was afraid of failing with the Jets... and he did. When he changed his thinking process, his coaching efforts outrivaled others.

Dick Vermeil took the head coaching position with the Philadelphia Eagles that year. Had he listened to his high school coach, Dick might still be employed in his father's automotive repair shop. However, his diligence and foresight led him to join Bill Parcells, Don Shula and Dan Reeves as the only coaches in NFL history to lead two different teams to Super Bowls.

The dapper Hank Stram signed on with the New Orleans Saints in 1976, defying the wishes of his high school coach who advised against a career in coaching. Stram, the first NFL coach to wear a microphone during a game, originated with the Dallas Texans/Chiefs from 1960—1974. An innovator and salesman, Coach Stram sold his players on the job that they were there to do. Congratulations, Coach Stram, for being the most winning coach in your 10-year history in the AFL with a record of 82-48-5.

Clint Murchison inducts Bob Lilly into the Ring of Honor. Photo by Bill Foster.

Our '76 season included the highlight of Don Meredith and Don Perkins joining Bob Lilly in the Cowboys Ring of Honor. Watching these stallions achieve their accolades was an inspiration. They were true champions who deserved this honor—pioneers who helped establish the Cowboys proud tradition. To me, the Ring encompasses their titles, triumphs and dedication. Their names overlooking Texas Stadium from the upper-deck facade will be a resounding voice for the history of the franchise to be heard by football fans forever.

Over the past two seasons, the Cowboys had a personnel turnover rate of 50 percent. This meant we had 20 players joining the team while the strength of the veterans remained a powerful core. Starting my 10th season, I still found our scouting formula to be a mystery. Joining the Cowboys in '76 were eight proficient players: defensive backs Aaron Kyle from Wyoming and Beasley Reece out of North Texas; running back Jim Jensen from

Iowa; Jim Eidson who attended Mississippi State; gifted Butch Johnson, a wide receiver from UC Riverside; tough guy Tom Rafferty from Penn State; Greg Schaum, a Michigan State defensive tackle; and defensive end Leroy Cook from Alabama.

Not only did we dream of a championship, we came to expect it. Once you win a Super Bowl, you want to win it again. We began the season with our efforts channeled towards winning the title.

Offensive line coach, Jim Myers, came from Texas A&M in 1962.

With a mixture of maturity and motivation, veterans and vitality, we won our first five games. Staubach was certainly on top of his game. You could say he was like our President. And who gets paid to protect the President? The Secret Service. That was my job—along with Fitzgerald, Nye, Lawless, Scott, Neely and Donovan. With his military training from the Marine Corps, Coach Myers instructed his offensive line with tact and perseverance. He was a disciplinarian. He taught us that if we didn't do our job and someone hurt the President, there would be hell to pay. Midway through this season, however, someone got to the President, stepped on his throwing hand and fractured a bone.

Towering Too Tall Jones.

Doomsday was dominant and destructive, allowing only one running back to gain 100 yards. Harvey Martin had an awe-inspiring season, with a record 15 quarterback sacks. Against the Giants, he 'Martinized' former teammate Craig Morton and preserved a last-second conquest. Too Tall was in the opposing QB's face the entire season. The special teams crew, featuring Hollywood Henderson and

Aaron Kyle, was indispensable. Our offense ran marathon drives that resulted in 296 points.

With an 11-3 record, we captured the East Division title for the 10th time in 11 seasons. We faced off with the Rams. From a numbers standpoint, we were favored to win because, in our previous two meetings, we outscored them 56-14. It was a competitively played game—a rollercoaster ride until the last few seconds. I guess the Rams were tired of getting beat in the playoffs as they took this one by a score of 14-12.

Coach Landry always believed his greatest teacher was *defeat*. "It builds character," he would constantly remind the team. After losing to the Rams—and to the Steelers in the previous Super Bowl—we should have been *masters of the game* and exploding with character.

★

One thing that was never at a loss in those days was the team's respect and honor for Coach Landry. The way he dressed, coached and carried himself on and off the field was the epitome of class. There wasn't a written bylaw for players to travel to games dressed in suits and ties. We just emulated the style of Coach Landry. There wasn't

Coach Landry was a natural-born leader. Photo by Bob Lilly.

a rule forbidding players to leave the bus or plane ahead of Coach Landry or his wife. We waited out of respect. And when I think about the gentle manner in which he regarded Alicia, his wife, I think it was the first time many players in that genre were exposed to such graciousness. It was a tremendous, unspoken lesson to many.

Coach Landry had sportsmanship, self-confidence and style. He was always considerate of his players and

190

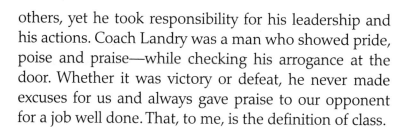

others, yet he took responsibility for his leadership and his actions. Coach Landry was a man who showed pride, poise and praise—while checking his arrogance at the door. Whether it was victory or defeat, he never made excuses for us and always gave praise to our opponent for a job well done. That, to me, is the definition of class.

★

So, did losing build character for the Dallas Cowboys that year? Honestly, from a co-captain's perspective, I saw how losing football games can build character in some players… while exposing the lack of it in others.

Titles and Tackling Other Challenges 1977

The NFL changed some rules this year that would affect the passing game and reduce the number of injuries. The headslap was outlawed (sorry Deacon Jones, but thank you, Jesus!). Defenders were allowed to make contact *only once* with eligible receivers. Offensive linemen were forbidden from thrusting their hands to an opponents head, neck or face. Wide receivers were barred from clipping.

★

During our usual training camp, we had relentless two-a-days where we worked on speed and conditioning. Staubach had the team's lowest body fat index of 9 percent. Mine was the next lowest at 11 percent. At the time, Coach Landry had a 265-pound limit on a player's weight. There was a *Fat Man's table* in the dining room where out-of-shape, unconditioned players would eat in full view of the coaching staff and players. Now I ask you—what other profession in America would you eat three meals a day in front of your bosses and your coworkers? Players never wanted to find themselves there, not only because of the humiliation but because the diet consisted of Jell-O, broth and other unidentifiable liquids. Luckily, since I always needed to gain weight, I never had to dine there. Back in his day, though, poor Willie Townes had daily reservations. He actually took it in great stride but the coaches were mystified when the pounds weren't melting away. A note to coaching staffs: tons of food can be stored underneath

a player's headboard in his dorm room.

By the time preseason ended, our team was solid muscle. Joining the Cowboys were seven players; quarterback Glenn Carano from Nevada;

Regardless of where he was, Willie Townes loved life. Photo by Bob Lilly.

Tony Hill, a wide receiver from Stanford; linebacker Guy Brown out of Houston; offensive linemen Andy Frederick from New Mexico and Temple's Jim Cooper; and David Stalls, defensive lineman from Northern Colorado. The most remarkable draft choice was Tony Dorsett, a University of Pittsburgh running back who was coached by the notable Johnny Majors. A Heisman Trophy winner, Dorsett added a new dimension to our attack and an element of unpredictability. Quarterback Steve DeBerg was a 10th-round draft pick but was released at the end of training camp. Steve went on to play 17 years in the NFL and I think his career was phenomenal.

For the first time in franchise history, we opened the season with eight consecutive victories before losing the next two against St. Louis and the Steelers. We closed the regular season with four consecutive victories, and then dropped the Bears 37-7 in a playoff game. The great Walter Peyton gained only 60 yards that day while our Charlie Waters grabbed three interceptions, a team playoff record.

Doomsday's defensive driving, led by Too Tall Jones, Harvey "Too Mean" Martin, Randy "the Manster" White, Bill Gregory and Jethro Pugh caused an unprecedented 53 sacks that season. Martin manhandled quarterbacks a record-setting 23 times.

On January 1, we accelerated to a 23-6 victory over the tough Minnesota Vikings and, once again, we found ourselves parked at the Super Bowl in New Orleans for the first championship game played in a domed stadium. Not only did we face Denver and their talented quarterback Craig Morton, but Broncomania was in our faces and at its finest. Orange Crush was the most popular beverage served in New Orleans that weekend. On second thought, maybe Orange Crush daiquiris were most admired.

Putting all emotions aside before a stadium crowd of 75,583 and a television viewing audience of 102 million, our game was confident and complete. Butch Johnson and Robert Newhouse had spectacular performances. Doomsday was in the dome causing eight crushing Bronco turnovers and limiting their passing to a mere 35 yards. I was ecstatic when Harvey Martin and Randy White shared the MVP award after our 27-10 victory.

★

At the end of the '77 season, Tony Dorsett had scored a remarkable 12 touchdowns and was selected Rookie of the Year. Chuck Howley became the fourth player to enter the Ring of Honor, joining Lilly, Meredith and Perkins. I remember Chuck as a devoted player and a solid team leader. He was unique and quiet. Although he wasn't very big, 225 pounds at best, his

Chuck Howley.
Photo by Bob Lilly.

presence was always felt on the field. Few players had his courage, character or strength. Another player I valued

195

Dave Edwards.
Photo by Bob Lilly.

was Dave Edwards. His nickname was "Fuzzy" yet, once the game clock started, he turned into a grizzly bear. His presence on the field was certainly known. He was never one to complain and never received his due. Individual recognition was out of our control.

In my opinion, this team was especially gifted and rich in talent. Roger Staubach. Preston Pearson. Robert Newhouse. Tony Hill. Billy Joe DuPree. Drew Pearson. Too Tall Jones. Jethro Pugh. Randy White. Harvey Martin. Bob Bruenig. Danny White. Charlie Waters. Cliff Harris. Benny Barnes. Hollywood Henderson. The most important thing was that we were a team and football is a team sport. From this perspective, we all received proper recognition because we won as a team and we lost as a team.

Charlie and Cliff—together like Butch and Sundance. Photo by Dallas Cowboys.

★

Football is a physical sport and, if you play the game for any length of time, injuries are inevitable. I sustained a knee injury midway through this season. During a pass play, my job was to bring the defensive end upfield and force them around Staubach. An opposing lineman dove for Roger but missed. However, the force of his helmet and shoulder pad smashed into the back of my knee. While my foot remained firmly planted in the turf, my body spun 360 degrees and I went down. The humiliation of being carried off the field wasn't nearly as great as the pain in my knee.

Every Monday we reviewed game films while the coaches evaluated each play and player. There were times when we felt like we'd lost the game by 100 points, even though we had won. Coaches graded and scored each performance as if it was a test. Throughout my career, I averaged scores in the upper 90s and 100s. Sometimes it was difficult being critiqued in front of teammates. It's comparable to a teacher exposing students and test scores—commenting on and correcting wrong answers. The experience was probably as degrading as sitting at the Fat Man's table. Some players took the criticism well while others could not. Being singled out for a mistake was sometimes embarrassing and some players were crudely teased if they took it personally. Some kept it bottled up or escaped the pain with drugs, alcohol or other forms of abuse. I dealt with mine through the power of prayer.

Classroom training. Photo by Bob Lilly.

It pained me to watch the film of my injury. I couldn't believe the way my body twisted around when I was hit. After the meeting, I certainly wasn't in a position to work out, so I went to the practice field and did my best to walk around the track. I remember Coach Landry jogged next to me asking, "How's the knee, Rayfield?" "It really hurts, Coach. I hope it's feeling better by Sunday," I replied. He looked me in my eyes and said, "It seems like you're walking alright. Just always remember, Rayfield, that running is *mental*." He continued jogging as I was left to wonder about his comment. *Did he think that I wasn't giving the game my all? Was this a test of mind over matter?* His statement challenged me that week as the trainers, through a series of knee draining, ice treatments and pain medications, did their best to get me back to 100 percent. Although the diagnosis was just a sprain, I knew there was something seriously wrong because each time they drained my knee (and the times were countless) there was blood in the fluid.

I played that Sunday and for the remainder of the season. It wasn't until after the Super Bowl and my sixth Pro Bowl appearance that the team doctors recommended immediate surgery for two torn cartilages. It was, by far, more than just a sprain.

★

The other injury I sustained in 1977 was heartache. Just after my knee surgery, Andrea came to me asking for a divorce. My heart broke for my children and for the dreams that would never come true. Growing up in a broken home, I tried everything in my power to prevent this from happening to my children. It was an awful time in my life and much more painful than my knee injury.

A Season Of Transitions
1978

The number of preseason games in the NFL was reduced this year from six to four while the regular season schedule increased from 14 to 16 games. Postseason playoffs were expanded to 10 teams as the NFL introduced three division champions and two wild-card entries from each conference. Wild-card teams would challenge one another.

Other changes to the game were the addition of a seventh official to judge the sidelines, and the effectiveness of instant replay was being studied. Now that would change the course of the game.

★

During the off-season, I was still hampered by leg pain. The doctors diagnosed severe nerve damage and scheduled my fourth operation. I entered my 12th training camp still recovering from surgery yet hopeful things would work out. It was the most mentally taxing training camp I ever attended.

Charting my progress.

The two-a-day practices caused pain and swelling in my knee so I gave the one-a-day's everything I could. With that much down time, I began to think about retirement although my beliefs in my playing ability remained strong.

Being sidelined at the start of the season was frustrating. When you've given your heart and soul to something for 12 years, it's tough taking the role of an onlooker. It felt as though time was passing me by. Having been a co-captain for so many years I continued motivating and leading the team as much as possible. It was good mental therapy. With the retirement of Ralph Neely, Coach Myers placed a tremendous challenge upon Andy Fredrick and Pat Donovan—young linemen taking the place of two veterans who had more than 20 years of combined tackling experience.

★

Howard Cosell, a controversial personality in sports broadcasting, announced our 38-0 Monday night victory over the Colts. Their 181 total yards without Bert Jones didn't hold a candle to our 587 yards. Another Cowboy fourth quarter, 34-24 comeback the next week against the Giants gave us our eighth consecutive victory over two seasons.

I regained my starting position with six games remaining in the season. Struggling with a 6-4 record, our playoff hopes seemed nearly impossible. My first game back was against Green Bay. It was great being in the saddle again. Confidence filtered through the offense as Staubach threw for 200 yards with DuPree, Dorsett and Newhouse scoring two touchdowns each. The 42-14 win kept us within one game of the Redskins and it began a six-game winning streak.

We entered the playoffs for the 12th time by facing the fired-up Falcons. A calm and collected Danny White rallied the team to a hard-fought 27-20 victory after a vicious hit left Staubach unconscious. Our next speed bump to the Super Bowl was, once again, the Rams. With the aptitude of their Jack Youngblood, Cody Jones, Tom Mack, Doug France, Dennis Harrah, Rich Saul, Rod Perry and Pat Thomas, we expected a bruising contest. But the bout was a 28-0 shutout as we proceeded to our fifth Super Bowl appearance in nine years.

★

Without a doubt, the 1978 Super Bowl was a classic featuring the most memorable players and teams of the 70s. An amazing match up between dominant teams. Staubach vs. Bradshaw. Tony Dorsett and Franco Harris. Tony Hill and John Stallworth. The Manster and Mean

Joe. Drew Pearson and Lynn Swann. Thomas Henderson and Jack Ham. Bob Bruenig and Jack Lambert. Too Tall and L.C. Greenwood. Cliff Harris and Mel Blount. Charlie Waters and Donnie Shell. Big Cat and Ray Pinney. Rafael Septien and Roy Gerela.

Tom Landry vs. Chuck Noll.

Doomsday II vs. the Steel Curtain.

The Dallas Cowboys vs. the Pittsburgh Steelers.

★

Both teams predicted they would win the title. The legendary George Halas orchestrated the pregame coin toss. Weeks prior to the game, we had designed a *Drew Pearson to Billy Joe DuPree pass play* from a reverse. What looked good on paper turned into trouble when a fumble occurred on the play. This turnover resulted in a Bradshaw-to-Stallworth touchdown pass. Late in the second quarter, Bradshaw was at his finest en route to surpassing Bart Starr's Super Bowl record of 253 passing yards. In the locker room at the half, we found ourselves down 21-14 but our spirits were alive with desire. We dominated the game through most of the third. In scoring position on the Pittsburgh 10, Roger found former St. Louis Cardinal tight end Jackie Smith wide open in the end zone and pitched a routine pass to him. I watched in disbelief as the ball deflected off Jackie and floated to the ground. A Rafael Septien field goal brought the score to 21-17.

The Steelers' offense continued displaying its talents with a Franco Harris score, followed by a Lynn Swann touchdown. However, we had 'Captain Comeback' on our side. True to form, Roger connected with Billy Joe DuPree for a touchdown with 2:23 left on the clock. Recovering an onside kick, we drove down the field once again. This time, with a meager 22 seconds remaining,

Staubach connected with Butch Johnson for our last touchdown.

The Steelers captured their third world title 35-31 and Bradshaw did a fine job directing his team. He passed for 318 yards and four touchdowns. Losing was disheartening for us, and my heart hurt for Jackie Smith. He was really hard on

My pained expression says it all.

himself after the game, but I imagine adversity made him a better player.

Besides, I never blamed Jackie for the loss. Teams win and lose *collectively*. That's just the way it is.

Out Of The Blue
1979

The '79 season marked the 20th anniversary for the Cowboys franchise. Our season opener took place on September 2 against the St. Louis Cardinals and their rookie running back Ottis Anderson. Winning the game at Busch Memorial Stadium that day awarded the Cowboys their 15th consecutive season opening victory. We never lost a season-opener during my 13-year career! Now, if we had won the last game of each season, that would have been a great success story!

On October 21, we met up with the Cardinals again—this time at Texas Stadium. The halftime ceremony honored many former players who were the foundation of our team. Since their retirement, most players were doing well while others were limited in finding decent, respectable employment. Some black players were struggling with cultural differences still affecting the workplace in America. But I applauded the efforts being made on both sides of the spectrum.

★

People called us America's Team. The name originated when NFL Films assigned the *America's Team* label to our 1978 highlight film. I know this reference is a turn-off for anti-Cowboy fans and some sports writers. When I first heard this slogan I initially thought, *Yes, only in America can opportunities or a dream like this come true.* America's a great country. But frankly, most players on the team, myself included, felt uncomfortable with this label. I know Coach Landry was. To me, we were a football team. I believe our namesake came about simply because many of our players were household names. Hayes. Pearson. Lilly. DuPree. Staubach. Meredith. Keep in mind—as football players *we* didn't come up with the America's Team name and it shouldn't have been held against us in such a negative manner. After all, people weren't critical of Green Bay for arrogantly being called *Title Town* and the Steelers didn't take any heat over the *Team of the Seventies* slogan.

We had recognition and fans in every NFL city in this country. Sure, they didn't want us to defeat their home team. I understood that. But they still had a fondness towards us. Personally, and I think I'm speaking for my colleagues, the promotional efforts behind the slogan were clever and certainly rewarding for us, but we never got caught up in being called America's Team. At the same time, I believe fans still affectionately refer to the early years of the Dallas Cowboys as America's Team... and probably always will.

★

With one year remaining on my contract, I was looking forward to this season. My knee had vastly improved because of another rigorous, off-season training program. While attending my 13th training camp, it dawned on me that I had been in training camp for *more than three years* of my 33-year-old life. In reality, three years is longer than today's NFL career average! That's a lot of sweat, sprints and two-a-days.

Camp was great considering the challenges I had faced the past two seasons. My knee felt good, I retained my quickness and I could still hold my own against the best ends in the NFL. So it hit me out of the blue when the coaches started Andy Frederick at right tackle. Nothing against Andy, but I had finished the past season as a starter and felt I had done my job. Most veterans on the team agreed because their starting positions were also challenged by second-team players.

★

Our defense was weakened by the retirement of Jethro Pugh. In a radical move, Too Tall left for a boxing career while strong safety Charlie Waters was sidelined with injuries. One thing was certain: I was thankful that I never had to challenge any Dallas defensive player, past or present, during a game. They tore some opponents apart like

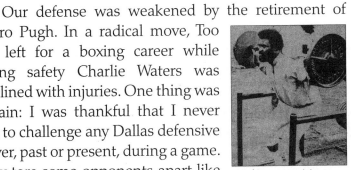

Working out at training camp.

tinker toys. Being on the receiving end during practice was brutal enough. Harvey Martin lived to punish and Too Tall was a beast. Jethro Pugh and Larry Cole ravaged their opponents.

On offense in 1979, Dorsett was hurt so rookie Ron Springs, a running back from Ohio State, provided talent and depth. Other new players contributing to the game were Robert Shaw from Tennessee, cornerback Aaron Mitchell from Las Vegas, Doug Cosbie a tight end from Santa Clara and Illinois tackle Bruce Thornton.

★

After our season-opening victory in St. Louis, our next two games over the 49ers and the Bears resulted in fourth-quarter victories. During the latter game, Walter Payton surpassed Rick Casares as Chicago's all-time leading rusher. *Way to go, Sweetness!* The next week we took a hit when Ozzie Newsome led Cleveland to a 26-7 victory.

At the halfway mark, our 7-1 record was a reflection of some well-fought games and gave us confidence. Staubach was stellar. Drew Pearson, Tony *The Thrill* Hill and Tony Dorsett each gained over 1,000 yards—a team first in the NFL.

At offensive tackle, Andy Frederick had been performing well in certain areas but was struggling to block some defensive ends. I was still ready and able to play when Coach Myers informed me that I was going to start the last three games. It looked as though we were going to fall short of being in the playoffs because the three remaining games were against New York, Philly and Washington. We were a game behind the Eagles and tied with the Redskins for second place. Destiny was in our hands. We had to compete.

Amazingly enough, we beat the odds. Prior to the Giants game, their coach, Ray Perkins, called his players to center field for the coin toss and made them *all* captains for the day. I thought it was a smart move but we psyched them out with a 28-7 victory. At Veterans Stadium the next week we battled the Eagles, their quarterback Ron Jaworski and a rapid running back named Wilbert Montgomery. United once again, we succeeded, 24-17.

With momentum, talent and a little luck, we faced the Redskins hoping to capture the NFC East. It was a contest of offense. It was Joe Theismann and John Riggins against Staubach, Springs and Newhouse. Facing a 34-21 deficit in the last four minutes, we rallied to a 35-34 victory.

Texas Stadium was the site for the NFC Championship showdown with the Rams. They brought a gritty team that included Vince Ferragamo, Wendell Tyler, Ron Smith, Billy Waddy, Nolan Cromwell and Jack Youngblood. We fought our way out of a 14-5 shortage thanks to a Ron Springs run in the third quarter and a Jay Saldi catch in the fourth. However, a late drive by the Rams clinched their 21-19 victory and the NFC title.

★

Almost four months after the playoff game, I returned home from my job at National Bank of Commerce to find 28 messages on my answering machine. That was unusual. While the recorder was rewinding, I called Georgia to check in with my mother and grandmother. "Things are fine here, Larry. No. Nobody's called here for you." After we said our goodbyes, I was eager to hear my messages. The first one was from Frank Luksa, a local sportswriter. *"Rayfield, it's imperative that you call me back immediately!"* Since 1969, when Frank first asked me how I was going to handle the Deacon, we had a respectable and honest relationship. The next urgent call was from Bob St. John, another local reporter. *"Hello, Rayfield. It's Bob. Please give me a call as soon as you get this message. It's important."* Thoughts in my mind began running rampant and a strange feeling began coiling in my stomach. On edge and anxious, I dialed Frank's number.

"Hey Frank. It's Rayfield. What's up?"

"The Cowboys just released a statement that they're not inviting you to training camp for the 1980 season," Frank explained. "Do you have any comment?"

I was totally shocked! After gathering my thoughts, I finally said, "That's news to me, Frank. I haven't been contacted by the organization. Are you *sure* that's a true statement? That's what they said?"

"Yeah it's true, Rayfield. That's what they said. I don't know why they'd let you go. It certainly doesn't make sense to me."

"Me neither, Frank. I'll call you back when I know something."

★

Even more apprehensive, I dialed Bob St. John's number.

"Hello, Bob. This is Rayfield Wright returning your call."

"Hey, Rayfield. I understand the Cowboys have released you. Is that true?" Bob asked.

"Well, Bob, Frank Luksa just asked me the same question and, like I told him, I haven't been contacted by Coach Landry or the organization. But I'll call you as soon as I have a comment."

Nothing made sense to me. After a few moments of gathering my thoughts, I called Coach Landry's office. His secretary, Marge, confirmed that Coach was still working and asked me to come on in.

★

The front office was usually a flurry of activity and excitement. However, on this occasion, it was hushed— an odd and eerie silence filled the hallways. I knocked on Coach Landry's door and he invited me in and offered a chair. After looking at each other for a few moments, I began to speak.

"Coach, I had a call this afternoon from Frank Luksa. Rumor has it that I'm not being invited back to training camp."

"That's true, Rayfield. The decision-makers want you to retire."

"With all due respect, Coach, I plan on retiring at the end of next year. This is the last year of my five-year contract! I don't understand."

"I'm sorry, Rayfield. This is what the organization has decided. Off-season training camp starts tomorrow and I'm telling the players that you won't be back. That you're retiring."

"Coach, I just finished the season as a starter! Why did this decision come up all of the sudden? And why didn't you or Coach Myers call me when the decision was made?"

"The decision came from *someone above me* and that's the way it is."

Throughout my entire life, no matter how upset or disappointed I became, I never argued with or raised my voice to an elder. I wanted to scream and shout at Coach Landry, but I certainly had too much respect for him to vent my frustrations in his office or towards him. Besides, it was obvious to me that he didn't make the final decision to let me go.

I stood to leave his office. When I got to the door, he said, "Rayfield, you've been the *best* offensive tackle the Dallas Cowboys have ever seen. I hope you have the highest football honors bestowed upon you one day. You'll deserve each and every one of them."

A difficult departure.
Photo by Geof Payne.

Choking back the tears, I turned to him and said, "Coach, it's been a great ride. You know I played healthy and I played hurt. Since 1967, I've given the game of football, my teammates and the Dallas Cowboys *everything* I had. As for the accolades, I'm not the one who makes those decisions. I've done my best with the talent God has given me. And I'm sorry it has to end this way."

In 1989, ten years after my retirement, Coach Landry departed the Cowboys on a *directive from the top* from new owner Jerry Jones. Regrettably, his exit was just as sudden as mine. I know in my heart that he felt the same deep emotions I experienced during my departure.

Coach Landry handled his abrupt departure with class and courage.

In a farewell to his players, Coach Landry summarized his feelings (and mine) when he told his team, *"The way you react to adversity is the key to success."*

Isn't that the most remarkable statement? You see, *adversity will defeat losers while inspiring winners.* Being successful in life is not about winning football games or

212

which team you're on.

And it certainly isn't about the *color* of your jersey.

It's about charging from the locker room and executing your game plan.

It's about tackling life's challenges to the best of your God-given abilities.

It's about listening for the *audible.*

More importantly, it's about how brightly your star shines in this glorious game we awaken to each day.

I'll say it once again.

Life remains a mystery.

So get your game on.

Stay up front and on the line.

And, by all means, enjoy the ride. You just don't know when your number will be called.

The Locker Room

I have played with the best of the best—the greatest of the greats. Here is a partial list of those paramount players from the Dallas Cowboys who I had the great fortune of teaming with. I've stated the first word that comes to mind when I recall the type of player or coach they were on the field… not off. The names in **bold** are players enshrined in the Ring of Honor at Texas Stadium. The star ★ represents Hall Of Fame inductees. To me, they are all stallions who have etched their names in Dallas Cowboys history.

Billy Joe "Duke" DuPree—*Hands*
Blaine Nye—*Respectful*
Bob "The Bullet" Hayes—*Speedo*
Bob "Mr. Cowboy" Lilly ★ *Man Among Men*
Burton Lawless—*Relentless*
Calvin Hill—*Physical*
Charlie Waters—*Watchful*
Chuck Howley—*Concrete*
Cliff "Crash" Harris—*Wrecking Crew*
Clint Murchison—*Smart*
Coach Tom Landry ★ *Systematic*
Coach Jim Myers—*Driven*
Cornell "Sweet Lips" Green—*Steady*
Coy Bacon—*Bold*
Craig Morton—*Technician*
D. D. Lewis—*Style*
Dan Reeves—*Scholar*
Dave "Fuzzy" Edwards—*A Rock*
Don "Dandy" Meredith—*Master Technician*
Don "Perk" Perkins—*Quick*
Drew "Clutch" Pearson—*Sensational*
Duane Thomas—*Graceful*
Ed "Too Tall" Jones—*Strength*
Forrest Gregg ★ *Experienced*
George Andrie—*Consistent*
Gil Brandt—*Clever*
Harvey "Martinizer" Martin—*Aggressor*
Herb Adderly ★ *Greatness*
Herb Scott—*Unexpected*
Jackie Smith ★ *Specialty*

Jay Saldi—*Surprising*
Jean "Fuge" Fugett—*Tenacious*
Jerry Tubbs—*Understanding*
Jethro "Buzz" Pugh—*Awesome*
John "Fitz" Fitzgerald—*Director*
John Niland—*Tactful*
Lance "Bambi" Alworth ★ *Smooth*
Lance Rentzel—*Fashioned*
Larry Cole—*Solid*
Lee Roy Jordon—*Mastermind*
Mel "Fro" Renfro ★ *Dependable*
Mike Ditka ★ *Heavy Hitter*
Mike Gaechter—*Forceful*
Pettis "Burch" Norman—*Aggressive*
Phil Clark—*Original*
Preston Pearson—*Smooth*
Ralph Neely—*Knowledgeable*
Randy "Manster" White ★ *A Hunter*
Robert "House" Newhouse—*Powerful*
Rodrigo Barnes—*A Searcher*
Roger "Rog" Staubach ★ *Determined*
Ron Springs—*Persistent*
Sims Stokes—*Fast*
Tex Schramm ★ *Shrewd*
Thomas "Hollywood" Henderson—*Player*
Willie "Baby Cakes" Townes—*Funny*
Tony "The Thrill" Hill—*Sweet*
Tony Dorsett ★ *Quickness*
Tony Liscio—*Teacher*
Walt "Puddin" Garrison—*Tough*

During my career, football was filled with rivalry, passion and excitement. I would like to salute and give thanks to the following players and coaches who exemplified their athletic skills on the field. As you read and reflect on these names, you will understand my thankfulness and what a tremendous honor and blessing it was for me to play the game in the midst of such greatness. The names in **bold** symbolize inductees in the Pro Football Hall of Fame in Canton, Ohio.

Ahmad Rashad	Vikings	Clarence Scott	Browns
Al Baker	Lions	Claude Humphrey	Falcons
Alan Page	Vikings	Cleveland Elam	49ers
Andy Russell	Steelers	Cliff Branch	Raiders
Archie Manning	Saints	Cody Jones	Rams
Art Shell	Raiders	Conrad Dobler	Cardinals
Bart Starr	Packers	Coy Bacon	Rams
Bert Jones	Colts	Curley Culp	Oilers
Bill Bergey	Eagles	**Dan Dierdorf**	Cardinals
Bill Bradley	Eagles	**Dan Fouts**	Chargers
Bill Curry	Colts	Dan Pastorini	Oilers
Bill Stanfill	Dolphins	**Dan Reeves**	Cowboys
Billy Johnson	Oilers	Daryle Lamonica	Raiders
Billy Kilmer	Redskins	**Dave Casper**	Raiders
Billy Thompson	Broncos	Dave Foley	Bills
Bob Baumhower	Dolphins	Dave Pear	Buccaneers
Bob Brown	Eagles	Dave Washington	49ers
Bob Griese	Dolphins	**Dave Wilcox**	49ers
Bob Grim	Vikings	David Hill	Lions
Bob Kuechenberg	Dolphins	**Deacon Jones**	Rams
Bob Lilly	Cowboys	Delvin Williams	49ers
Bob Trumpy	Bengals	Dennis Harrah	Rams
Bob Vogel	Colts	Dick Anderson	Dolphins
Bob Young	Cardinals	**Dick Butkus**	Bears
Bobby Bell	Chiefs	Dick Jauron	Lions
Bobby Bryant	Vikings	Diron Talbert	Redskins
Brad Van Pelt	Giants	**Don Maynard**	Jets
Bruce Laird	Colts	**Don Shula**	Dolphins
Bruce Taylor	49ers	Donnie Shell	Steelers
Bruce Van Dyke	Steelers	**Doug Atkins**	Saints
Bubba Smith	Colts	Doug English	Lions
Buck Buchanan	Chiefs	Doug France	Rams
Bud Grant	Vikings	Dwight White	Steelers
Carl Eller	Vikings	**Earl Campbell**	Oilers
Cedrick Hardman	49ers	Ed Budde	Chiefs
Charley Taylor	Redskins	Ed Flanagan	Lions
Charley Young	Eagles	Ed White	Vikings
Charlie Johnson	Eagles	**Elvin Bethea**	Oilers
Charlie Joiner	Chargers	Emmitt Thomas	Chiefs
Charlie Sanders	Lions	Ezra Johnson	Packers
Chip Myers	Bengals	Floyd Little	Broncos
Chris Hanburger	Redskins	Forest Blue	49ers
Chuck Foreman	Vikings	**Forrest Gregg**	Packers
Chuck Muncie	Saints	**Fran Tarkenton**	Vikings
Chuck Noll	Steelers	**Franco Harris**	Steelers

Fred Biletnikoff	Raiders	**Joe Namath**	Jets
Fred Carr	Packers	Joe Washington	Colts
Fred Dean	Chargers	John Brockington	Packers
Fred Dryer	Rams	John Dutton	Colts
Gale Gillingham	Packers	John Gilliam	Vikings
Gale Sayers	Bears	John Hadl	Chargers
Gary Garrison	Chargers	**John Hannah**	Patriots
Gene Upshaw	Raiders	John Jefferson	Chargers
Gene Washington	49ers	**John Mackey**	Colts
George Allen	Rams	**John Riggins**	Redskins
George Blanda	Raiders	**John Stallworth**	Steelers
George Kunz	Falcons	John Zook	Falcons
Glen Edwards	Steelers	**Johnny Unitas**	Colts
Greg Landry	Lions	Ken Anderson	Bengals
Greg Pruitt	Browns	Ken Burrough	Oilers
Hank Stram	Chiefs	Ken Ellis	Packers
Harold Carmichael	Eagles	**Ken Houston**	Oilers
Harold Jackson	Rams	Ken Stabler	Raiders
Harry Carson	Giants	Kim Bokamper	Dolphins
Haven Moses	Broncos	L.C. Greenwood	Steelers
Henry Childs	Saints	**Lance Alworth**	Cowboys
Herb Adderly	Packers	Larry Brooks	Rams
Herb Mulkey	Redskins	Larry Brown	Redskins
Isaac Curtis	Bengals	**Larry Csonka**	Dolphins
Isaiah Robertson	Rams	**Larry Little**	Dolphins
J.D. Hill	Bills	**Larry Wilson**	Cardinals
J.T. Thomas	Steelers	Lawrence McCutcheon	Rams
Jack Gregory	Giants	Lee Brooks	Cardinals
Jack Ham	Steelers	**Lee Roy Selmon**	Buccaneers
Jack Lambert	Steelers	**Lem Barney**	Lions
Jack Reynolds	Rams	Lemar Parrish	Bengals
Jack Rudnay	Chiefs	**Len Dawson**	Chiefs
Jack Tatum	Raiders	Len Hauss	Redskins
Jack Youngblood	Rams	Leon Gray	Oilers
Jackie Slater	Rams	**Leroy Kelly**	Browns
Jackie Smith	Cowboys	Louie Kelcher	Chargers
Jake Scott	Dolphins	Louis Wright	Broncos
James Harris	Rams	Lydell Mitchell	Colts
James Lofton	Packers	Lyle Alzado	Broncos
Jan Stenerud	Chiefs	**Lynn Swann**	Steelers
Jeff Siemon	Vikings	Marv Hubbard	Raiders
Jeff Van Note	Falcons	**Marv Levy**	Bills
Jerome Barkum	Jets	Marvin Powell	Jets
Jerry Logan	Colts	Matt Blair	Vikings
Jerry Sherk	Browns	**Mel Blount**	Steelers
Jerry Sisemore	Eagles	Mel Gray	Cardinals
Jim Bertelsen	Rams	**Mel Renfro**	Cowboys
Jim Carter	Packers	Mercury Morris	Dolphins
Jim Finks	Bears	**Merlin Olsen**	Rams
Jim Hart	Cardinals	Mike Boryla	Eagles
Jim Langer	Dolphins	Mike Curtis	Colts
Jim LeClair	Bengals	**Mike Ditka**	Bears
Jim Mitchell	Falcons	**Mike Haynes**	Patriots
Jim Otis	Raiders	Mike Lucci	Lions
Jim Otto	Raiders	Mike Pruitt	Browns
Jim Tyrer	Chiefs	Mike Reid	Bengals
Jim Youngblood	Rams	Mike Reinfeldt	Oilers
Jimmy Johnson	49ers	Mike Thomas	Redskins
Joe DeLamielleure	Bills	Mike Wagner	Steelers
Joe Ehrmann	Colts	**Mike Webster**	Steelers
Joe Greene	Steelers	Milt Morin	Browns
Joe Lavender	Redskins	Monte Jackson	Rams

Rayfield Wright's
GAME SUMMARY

Years	Playoff Years	Co-Captain Years	Super Bowls	Season Openers	All-Pro	Pro Bowls	Offensive Lineman of the Year	Season Record
1967	★			Win				9-5
1968	★			Win				12-2
1969	★			Win				11-2-1
1970	★	★	V	Win				10-4
1971	★	★	VI*	Win	★			11-3
1972	★	★		Win	★	★	★	10-4
1973	★	★		Win		★		10-4
1974		★		Win	★	★	★	8-6
1975	★	★	X	Win	★	★		10-4
1976	★	★		Win		★		11-3
1977	★	★	XII*	Win		★		12-2
1978	★	★	XIII	Win				12-4
1979	★			Win				11-5
13	12	9	5	13	4	6	2	137-48-1

*Super Bowl Victories

Dallas Cowboys 1st Anniversary Team—1985.
Dallas Cowboys All Decade Team of the 1970s.
Dallas Cowboys Ring of Honor—Texas Stadium—Inducted 2004.
Hall of Faith Award—Athletes International Ministries—1977.
Hall of Fame—Griffin, Georgia. Inducted 1974.
Hall of Fame—Fort Valley State College. Inducted 1983.
Hall of Fame—State of Georgia. Inducted 1988.
Heroes of Football™—Inducted 2000.
NFL All Super Bowl Team—1990.
NFL Legends Award—1990.
NFL Alumni "Ring of Honor" Dallas Chapter—2003.
Pat Summerall & John Madden's—Best of the Dallas Cowboys 1995.
Texas Black Sports Hall of Fame—Inducted 2002.
Texas Sports Hall of Fame—Inducted 2005.

★*Dallas Morning News*—Rated Rayfield Wright #6 (of 12) Top Team Sport Players in Dallas/Fort Worth history—2004.

★*Fort Worth Star Telegram*—Rated Rayfield Wright #20 (of 40) of the Most Important People in Dallas Cowboy's history—1999.

★*Sports Illustrated*—Rated Rayfield Wright #42 (of 100) of the Top 20th Century Sport Figures from the State of Georgia—2000.

★

The End Zone

A message to all who have read this book,

Looking back through the chapters of my life, I can clearly see that God has a master plan for my life—just as he has orchestrated yours. I hope this part of my life's story lifted your spirits and delivered the gift of hope.

Remember that God has called you for a divine reason. Look inside and find your purpose. Stay in the game, run the race and keep the faith so that, when it's over, you will receive the crown of glory that has been laid up for you.

I pray that God will bless and keep you; that his face will shine upon you and be gracious; and that he will lift up his countenance upon you and give you peace. Numbers 6:24-26.

God Bless.

I remain,
Larry Rayfield Wright

★